The Left Handed Cannibal

The Life & Writings of Myron Stanley Nixon, 1919-2000

Author, Horticulturalist, Plant Geneticist,
Anthropologist & Postman

As Originally Written by:
Myron Stanley Nixon, A. S., B. S.
Chesterfield, Illinois

As Collated & Narrated by:
Joseph M. Nixon, Ph. D., RPA
Hemet, California

With Generous Contributions by
Family, Friends & Acquaintances

authorHOUSE®

AuthorHouse™
1663 Liberty Drive
Bloomington, IN 47403
www.authorhouse.com
Phone: 1-800-839-8640

First published by AuthorHouse   10/22/2009

ISBN: 978-1-4490-2473-4 (e)
ISBN: 978-1-4490-2471-0 (sc)
ISBN: 978-1-4490-2472-7 (hc)

Library of Congress Control Number: 2009910494

Printed in the United States of America
Bloomington, Indiana

This book is printed on acid-free paper.

CONTENTS

PREFACE

The following is an excerpt from an article that appeared in the North American Fruit Explorers journal, the *Pomona,* first issued in 1967 and still available[1]. The anonymous author acquired and read many of the original issues of that journal. Doing so kindled in him the spirit of those who lived and worked through the vagaries of both the Great Depression and shortly thereafter, WWII, and who survived the many hardships brought by those trying days. He expresses a longing for their simpler, more straightforward times, for days when, in his opinion, more humanistic values dominated our culture. He writes of its contributors (Anonymous 2003):

> There exists a sense of profoundness in their words as they recounted their memories of an age that I, frankly, never experienced and a state of innocence I suppose I never had. . . I'll just say that I feel blessed to have my life enriched by the words of those whom tread this earth before me.

In the mid 1920s, a combination of over eager optimism combined with rampant speculation culminated at the end of the decade in a calamitous stock market crash. Beginning on October 24, 1929 (Thursday), the market started a steep decline that prompted rampant, panic based, selling that, on the following Tuesday, October 29, 1929 (Black Tuesday), sent fiscal shock waves into the investment community. Financial centers teetered and then finally collapsed. Once holding sway over a fat empire, the importance and influence of the financial centers fell into atrophy and the US economy staggered, reeled, and then fell. The small percentage of the population that once controlled this fragile house of dollars suffered inestimable losses as the fickle breezes of capitalism swept away the hollow infrastructure built by those same investors. In the end, economic realism trumped greed.

Those that were not members of that financial club, including those that farmed or worked in factories, or maintained everyday jobs, felt the repercussions of this economic fallout in combination with an unprecedented drought in the

---

1   Their webpage (http://www.nafex.org/) indicates that a group of amateurs formed NAFEX (North American Fruit Explorers) in 1967 and it is still operational. They now boast some 3000 members with an international representation. Their journal, the *Pomona,* is still published and available and their combined amateur-professional membership continues their active, hands on research into development of more productive, better tasting, and more appealing natural fruits and nuts.

years from about 1931 to 1938, years that in retrospect we call the Great Depression. While the lost fortunes of the Rockefellers and the Vanderbilts made headline news (assuming you could afford a newspaper), the common man endured quietly. Many people, sometimes entire industries, lost their jobs. In response the government intervened in sectors of business where it had never before tread. The Works Progress Administration, for example, funded intern programs employing carpenters, stone masons, road workers, artists, writers, and others whose work built much of our present infrastructure.

Those not benefitting from the federal assistance – including those who worked the land - turned back to it for support, becoming dependent on it just like their ancestors before them. They planted small gardens and re-learned how to survive on home grown sustenance. Those who had no land turned to relatives and friends who did; and those who did – while having little to begin with – shared their meager lot with friends and neighbors and kinfolk. Retreating to a barter based economy, the common people traded whatever goods and services they had for fresh produce, grain, nuts, berries, and other fruits of the land.

Ironically, and perhaps an echo of the American spirit that we all have inherited, family values, sharing, and being a good neighbor resurfaced in the face of common crisis that showed no signs of abating. But soon after about 1940, the US could no longer avoid the conflict that raged in Europe. Entering into the fray, whether by choice or simply seeking relief, Americans in the US momentarily set aside the grief and suffering of the Depression in the face of yet another common crisis, one that diverted attention from growling stomachs and bare supper tables, to the need for a global response to authoritarianism.

Small farm communities, already used to giving, were asked once more to sacrifice, this time not just the fruits and vegetables so painstakingly tended in their fields and gardens, but now their sons and daughters, to a fight in conflict half a world away. As insulated as these small farm enclaves might have seemed, events now thrust them directly onto the global stage and they sent their sons and daughters into countries that until that time they only knew from geography lessons. The ancestors of many of these peaceful agrarians, after all, came from those very countries in Europe that now were threatened. With an engrained sense of giving anyhow, it seemed almost natural to offer up generous portions of what little they had.

DEDICATION

This work is dedicated to common people everywhere. To men and women who have both dreams and the uncommon determination to achieve them. While being the story of one such man, this is the story of all men and women who dream and believe and make their dreams come true. It promotes family values, it applauds determination, it recognizes hard work and the spirit of accomplishment fostered in a society where free choice is the norm. This work derives from, and is dedicated to, the cumulative intellect and drive of everyday men and women who strive to achieve their dreams through their families, their lives, and their children.

ACKNOWLEDGEMENTS

Friends, family, coworkers, cousins, acquaintances, all contributed to this story. Each in his own way and each to his own degree, are part of the saga related here. I appreciate and acknowledge the help and assistance from everyone. To those of you who provided anecdotes, shared memories, suggested subtle changes, and tendered support, I offer thanks and wish only that there were ample opportunity to recognize all. Short of that, rest well with the satisfaction of knowing that your memories and your contributions were critical to the overall telling of this tale. And, as Dad might have quipped: "That and a quarter would get you a cup of coffee". I appreciate all your help.

I especially acknowledge the time and the effort by BFF who read and commented on this manuscript with a keen eye to historical accuracy and a kind heart to fondness of memory.

INTRODUCTION

Here you will find an account of the life of the contemporary American Anthropologist: Myron Stanley Nixon, late of Chesterfield, Illinois. You will not find his name in esteemed Anthropology journals. Nor will you find him among any list of laureates. He neither wanted nor sought such recognition.

During his involuntary military service as an enlisted "grunt" he declined field promotion to officer status on more than one occasion. I have no doubt that his reaction to any offer of academic recognition would have been met with the same, polite "No thanks" that probably preceded his walking away from the shiny golden bars of a Lieutenant.

This account relates the sequence of events that shaped Dad's life with an emphasis on his education and his writings. Time dictates that the perspective for this story must be through the eyes of his daughter, his son, his family, his friends, and his acquaintances. Although their words and memories comprise the warp and weft of the fabric, wherever possible his own words are included, shading more of his personality into the finished weaving.

I begin this version of his story after much thought and many changes of mind, after many false starts, and after many conversations with those very family and friends. I write now because maturity has allowed a more clear understanding of the support that Mom and Dad (Myron Stanley and Opal Faye Long-Nixon) provided to my sister, to me, and to the entire community in which we lived. That, combined with realism tempered by experience, has culminated in this effort to recount the story of this son of Chesterfield.

As editor and narrator I ask that you be patient when I recount seemingly unrelated stories and facts. They are not pointless filler and they are not commercials. I have inserted them as needed to maintain chronological order, to fill in blanks in time in which Dad wrote nothing, or to keep the narrative orderly, continuous and flowing.

At the beginning of each chapter is a description of the works that immediately follow, with observations about their style, motivation, date of authorship when known, placement in time, and other pertinent details. Also, scattered throughout the narrative are supporting documents such as letters from colleges, opinions from other authors about Dad or his work, Instructors' comments, grades, literary suggestions, and other material. I placed these where they clarify, explain, or otherwise illustrate his story.

With regard to copyrights: As far as I am concerned, all of this material belongs to Dad. You are free to use any or all of it as you want as long as you truly believe he would approve. I am sure that were you to leave that decision up to him, he would shrug his shoulders and say "Well, that's up to you" anyhow.

Dad did not date many of his writings at the time he penned them. The serial and relentless Professors he encountered as he worked his way through college taught him that habit. Often needing material to fulfill class assignments, he wrote some of these pieces from memory and the date of actual authorship does not match the subject matter. As an example, he wrote *Coming to America* in 1995 and within it, he discusses events that span from 1863 to 1951. These temporal mismatches are noted where they occur. Using the general time frame explained below, I have attempted to group these dateless works into realistic contexts that would reflect his thinking.

Finally, the few editorial notes I have added to explain, to clarify, to illustrate, *etc.*, appear in brackets when inserted into original text so that the rare mechanical guidepost is readily distinguishable from his written intent.

I. AT THE OPTOMETRIST

One of the more difficult problems in assembling this manuscript has been accounting for my Father's life from approximately 1948-1949. Being born near the end of 1946, those were the days of my earliest childhood memories, when my two or three year old mind was just recognizing the advantages I might gain by remembering things. I have tried to organize events chronologically, to put things reasonably one before the other, in an effort at reconstruction.

Much the way the Optometrist might ask "Which is better, A or B", I looked at specific events and asked: Which was first? This involved isolating the earliest events, identifying their consequences, and moving through time searching for connections between one identifiable event and the next. The result was to place things into a hopefully representative time order reflecting fairly distinct phases of Dad's life. Generally these included the ancestry that preceded him, his home days as a boy, the coming of WWII and his military service, his discharge and landing a government job, their (with Mom) coming into the ownership of land, acquisition and improvements to their own home, having and raising children their way, and finally his attendance at college.

I made the decision to use this approach fully understanding that its basis is in events determined by Dad himself. It recognizes that in the flow of actual life, these changes may have been unconscious to him. He did not, for example, decide one day to culture blackberries, waking up and announcing "Today I am going to grow blackberries". Rather, the various stages of his life developed through unintentional expressions of his own personal interests exercised through his freedom of choice, in this case, leading to blackberries.

Using this approach, this narrative begins with a look at the origins of the families of both Mother (Opal Faye Long of Alton, Illinois) and Father (Myron Stanley Nixon of Chesterfield, Illinois). Unfortunately, no one in the family knows much about their early lives until they met, apparently right after his discharge from the military. Neither of them ever spoke freely of their initial meeting, told any stories about going to a picnic, or a party, or any significant courtship event. Despite repeated attempts, my sister and I managed to garner only a very sketchy understanding of their early days together. As a result, nearly all the story of their courtship is lost.

Fortunately, at the nagging insistence of my sister and me, Dad undertook to record the story of his parents and grandparents, of their beginnings in Croule (Crewell, Crewelle, other spp.?), Lincolnshire, England, and their trek across a cold ocean to a new country that promised land, opportunity, and prosperity. The text of this document which he titled *Coming to America* spans from October of 1863 until April of 1951.

Dad's account of this journey across the Atlantic is an interesting story on its surface. But within its lines - sometimes expressed and other times simply implied - are the lessons of his Grandmother and Mother that would shape his later development.

First there was the importance of land, critical both to these early immigrants from the Continent and to Dad once in possession of his own property. Second were the natural resources that abounded on the land if you knew where to look. Fruits, berries, nuts, all contributed to a diet gathered and processed by a protectively tight family unit, the third element of basic values linked directly to Dad's boyhood. This connectivity and closeness extended to others in his family as well as to other local families, expressed no more unselfishly than when relatives – who had nothing themselves - took in kinfolk and neighbors who had even less.

And much later - education. Dad's words recall the concerted efforts made by his Mother and Grandmother to absorb whatever they could from the limited educational opportunities offered in the one room, rural schoolhouses of the day. But with hard times, the need for labor during harvest periods, the perpetual quest for food, and other demands, the desire for education outstripped the opportunities. But the seed of desire so planted would bloom when opportunity finally arrived.

The value of land, the bounty of the resources it produced, the closeness of family and friends, and a genuine thirst for learning were central to the teachings of his boyhood. Whether he realized it or not, together these values shaped his attitude toward life. All are reflected in this short, but revealing, piece about family origins.

Chapter III dates to the period beginning in November 1941 when Dad joined the Army and extending about 1945 when the service discharged him. This short section, titled *War Stories*, contains several pieces written later in life that reflect his experiences while serving in the Army. These he wrote after the fact and not during his military service; he wrote them from his memories. Like so many other veterans of WWII, for years after separation from the military, Dad remained totally silent about his experiences. In his case, though, writing provided an outlet and he finally 'opened up' a little through the medium of written humor.

For her own unexpressed reasons, Mom also said little about her origins. On reflection, she shared Dad's dream of a place of their own. Having grown up with four sisters, she wanted a house that she could keep her own way and in which she could raise and nurture her own children, also her own way. Chapter IV, titled *This Land is My Land*, describes events in their lives from about 1949-1950 and focuses on their early years together when they acquired their property in Chesterfield and became – to their mutual and long awaited satisfaction – 'landed'. That shared dream did come true for them. The years of hard work, the unrelenting poverty, and the continuous day to day struggles they experienced, however, do not appear in any of his writings.

Living on their own property and in their own home, they launched into an improvement blitz that included both my younger sister and me, willingly or not. When I was a boy, I went through the usual dinosaur stage, fascinated by the bones of these giants illustrated in the (then) politically correct textbooks. I wondered how the world might have looked back then, the animals, the plants, the weather, the earthquakes, the mountains just growing . . . But, if your parents subscribed to the Time-Life series, then like steaming hot chocolate plopped onto your bowl of already wonderful fudge ice cream, you also got the "artists rendition" of their appearance, their prey, their habits, their habitat, all of it -- in full color. My mind could look at those images and see the creatures that lived, thought, ate, nested, hatched eggs, cared for their young, migrated, had life cycles – massive creatures that actually lived! When I looked at those illustrations my mind could see the living creatures.

Sometime later, when I was a teenager, I was shocked when I finally saw an actual life sized dinosaur skeleton in Vernal, Utah, at Dinosaur National Park. Shocked because I was unable to look at these dry, sterile, and lifeless bones and visualize a living creature in my mind as I had done with the Time-Life representations.

One of the fix up projects that Dad undertook shocked me similarly. I must have been five or so when, returning home from school one day and opening the front door, I saw nothing but stringers across the floor. Without a word of warning, Dad had removed everything that day. There was no insulation, no flooring, no floor covering, nothing but the dirt beneath the house staring up between the silent 2x10 sentinels. Like the ribs of the dinosaur, my mind could not connect the image of those bare boards and sterile earth to thoughts of a happy family sitting together in the evening listening to the radio. I could not see life represented by either those stark white dinosaur bones or the bare stringers across that floorless living room.

While we were doing various improvement projects inside the house, Dad was exploring the acreage. First, he removed dead and seriously ill plants, burning the residue frequently. As a family, we often roasted hot dogs and – of course - marshmallows around the brush fire as it burned down to its evening embers. Next, he planted in areas that, like his father before him, he cleared by hand (or hands, if you include mine). As things settled into a routine and time permitted, Dad began experimenting with local fruit and nut bearing plants including mulberries, black walnuts and pecans. No doubt the lessons of his Grandmother about the bounties of nature and respect for their source were at the basis of his efforts to increase the natural health of these plants and, thereby, their edible yields. Nonetheless, this began a lifelong interest of his in plant propagation and genetics which is explored in Chapter V, titled *Why Plant That Tree?* This period spanned from approximately 1950 to 1963.

Although initially based in practicality and survival, the experimental elements of his botanical passion now were free to develop. As people do in the rural Midwest, Dad began to talk to others with the similar interests. Soon the botanical skills he enjoyed so much began to improve; his local reputation began to accumulate, and; more and more often others sought his advice about plant related issues. His acumen at his hobby soon expanded his circle of acquaintances to include staff at the local universities, nursery men, and others even more physically distant. As their contact group expanded, it became increasingly clear that communication among often distant like-minded fellows required not only occasional meetings and discussions of mutual interests in person, but also expression of thoughts and experiences in the pages of the journals that spontaneously developed to foster communication within their membership. Chapter VI, which I call *Discovering an Audience: INTA, NAFEX, & Pomona (1963-1973)*, focuses on this developing written network of people with similar interests.

Inspired by active participation in these organizations, by writing as a formal means of communication, and by two children who were as relentless as he was about going to school, he finally consented to take a college course. Chapter VII, *School Days (Again)*, looks at his involvement in higher education for the next seven years, from acceptance to Lewis and Clark College in 1973 to graduation from SIU Edwardsville in 1980. Many of the narratives to follow come from his experiences at this time.

Now a college graduate with training and experience in writing, Dad was in a position to select his topics and to preserve in text those things he thought worth the effort. Chapter VIII, titled *Too Soon We Are Old*, reflects the period from 1980 to 2000. Although the output was not prodigious, it is some of his best work. Much of it, also, he wrote as reflections on earlier events in his life utilizing his now trained skills in writing.

The contents of Chapter IX, titled *All Grandpa! All the Time!* range across the calendar from the year 2000 to a more recent piece that harks back to his *Pomona* days. I provide the following table as a map that visually shows the sequencing of events in Dad's life. Again, the specific ordering was frequently decided by asking: Which was earlier, "A" or "B", and aligning things accordingly. I hope you have good glasses and can read the fine print. Otherwise, you better see an optometrist.

Table 1: Generalized Time Line, Myron S. Nixon

<u>Date</u>   <u>Event</u>

?   October 6, 1863-1951, family origins, Lincolnshire, England
May 20, 1890   Viola Mae born, Dad's Mother
Feb 4, 1912   Viola married Harley Nixon; children Melba Lucile (Jul 12, 1913),
                                 Ruby Mae (Feb 12, 1916), Myron Stanley (Nov 25, 1919)

Feb 14, 1920   Harley dies of pneumonia, Dad age 2½ mo
1929   At age 10, Dad begins to hunt & trap to help support family
1931-1938   Great Depression
1937   Dad graduates from Chesterfield High School
1939   Work at Alton Box Board until drafted into Army (WWII)

Nov 5, 1941   Army days
Dec 7, 1941   Pearl Harbor
Nov 5, 41 – Jul 42   Stationed in New Zealand and Australia
Jul 1942   Bivouac in Fijii Islands/defense & jungle commando training
Jun 1945   Discharge (bronze star, 2 purple hearts, numerous campaign and expeditionary
                                 ribbons), civilian again, return to Illinois

May 31, 1946   Married to Faye Long
Dec 26, 1946   Son, Joseph, born
May 25, 1948   Daughter, Gale, born
1949-1950   Move into the Middlecoff place just east of Chesterfield
1949?   Restaurant operator; Post Office Employee; purchase Chesterfield Home

1950   Moved into Chesterfield homestead
Apr 1951   Dad's Mother died, colon cancer
1950-1953   Why plant that tree; fruit and nut experimentation
1963-1973   Discovering an audience
1960-1973   INTA, NAFEX, and botanical interests

1973   Accepted, Lewis & Clark Junior College
1973-1976   Liberal Arts (?) student, Lewis & Clark College
Jun 1977   Graduate Lewis & Clark, Associate of Science degree
1976-1980   SIU Edwardsville, Anthropology Department
Jun 1980   Graduate SIU, Bachelor of Science degree in Anthropology

2000   Requiem

II. A TERRIBLE COLD PLACE (1863-1951)

Through the years, my sister and I learned little about Mom and Dad's past, about their lives before they met, or even about their meeting. We know that Mom was from Alton, Illinois, and that she had four sisters: Ruth, Wilma (everyone knows her as "Wimp"), Thelma, and Bernice. She did share a few childhood stories with my sister who astutely noted that every memory of childhood that she (Mom) related, she did so in a laughing, happy manner. In spite of financial difficulties and seemingly poverty-level conditions, Mom remembers a happy childhood, always giggling when sharing anecdotes. Only the eyes of a child – Mom as a child – could look back at those lean days and selectively recall the memories that lit up her face as she joyfully relived them with my sister.

Later in life everyone in the family knew Reba Weimers, Mom's mother, as "Grammy". Few of us ever met her husband "Pappy"; to our group regret, he died when most of us were still young, many not yet born. Being only about three or so then, I have vague memories of a tall man in a dark business suit of the day. I remember sitting on his knee and fishing around in his coat pockets where he had always hidden a stick of Juicy Fruit which belonged to the most curious among the grandkids. I remember a kind man who tended – in retrospect with great reserve - to tolerate the often disruptive and sometimes destructive activities of children that visited them. Pappy Long had at least one brother, Bob, who has a role in this story later.

Grammy and Pappy raised these five girls in a small house in Alton. My sister, Gale, remembers one day when she and Mom actually drove by her old Alton home. It was not far from the apartment where Grammy lived toward the end of her life. Gale continues: Again, my memories are hazy, but I picture a very small one-story (not big enough to be referred to as a ranch), wood frame house situated at the bottom of a hill with a postage stamp front yard, surrounded by other similar houses.

My sister sarcastically reasons that it was inevitable that Mom would have a husband who belonged to the Nut Growers Association, as she had personal experience with walnuts as a teenager. Mom, Bernice, Thelma, Ruthie, Wimp, and at least one extra friend met in their one bathroom (remember the family consisted of Grammy, Pappy, and five daughters). They filled the sink with hot water and as many walnuts as they could gather and used the walnut-dyed water to darken their hair. Unanticipated problems included a black sink and walnut-stained hands.

Giggling on, Mom related further adventures in the Long household on Saturday night. Every Saturday afternoon, all five girls began arguing about who would wear which dress to complement their newly dyed walnut-stained coiffures to the dance that evening. Grammy and Pappy crammed all five girls into the back seat of their car and headed for the dance hall. Pappy lined up his girls in chronological order at the side of the dance floor to show them off, as he was very proud of them. He and Grammy then proceeded to dance the night away. At some point during the evening, all the girls joined the adults in circle dancing, swinging and swirling, laughing and bouncing. Pappy danced one dance with each daughter before the evening came to a close.

My sister continues with Mom's recollections. I am not sure if they had more than one bed for all five girls, because each of them shared stories about all five of them sleeping in one bed, three at the top, and two at the bottom. They often had one or more friends spending the night with them in the one bed. When Thelma invited a plump friend to a sleepover, the other four ousted them to the floor. They attempted to make a policy that they would only invite skinny friends over for the night.

When my sister and I were children, all of Mom's sisters and their families lived in or around Alton with the exception of Thelma who moved to Florida some time earlier. From the family farm in Chesterfield, Alton was a forty five minute drive. Grammy lived near Alton most of her life. Paul Weimers, her last husband, was a dairy farmer from Bethalto, Illinois; he was deceased when she died. When we were small, our family frequently made the short journey to visit both Grammy and Paul and Mom's sisters and their families who remained in Alton; we took family outings.

Dad had two sisters, Ruby and Melba, both of whom spent most of their lives in the Godfrey and nearby Wood River and Bethalto, Illinois, area. Together with Alton, these communities constituted the major settlement on the Illinois side of the Mississippi River across from the St. Louis metro area. It also took about forty five minutes to get to their homes from Chesterfield and they were all in the same direction, frequently turning what was to be a simple family outing into a pan-family visiting bonanza.

Dad's father died when he was just a few months old, leaving him with his Mother and Grandmother, and those two sisters. Over the years they spoke infrequently about their early life other than to mention occasionally that they were very poor and that they depended on nature to provide much of their subsistence. Whenever we passed by the old farmstead, Dad would always point it out and reminisce about gardening, about the fruits and vegetables on which they depended, and about hunting to supplement their diet once Dad was of age to do so.

One of Dad's most frequently told stories relates directly to this harvesting of natural foodstuffs. It seems that when he was small – recall that he was the youngest of three children – Mother would outfit them for a day of picking blackberries. Each child received a pail that as Dad would say was "pro-rated". The biggest child got the biggest bucket and the littlest – him – got the smallest. Mother's rule was that you could pick at your own speed and you could pick whenever wanted but you could not come home to supper until your bucket was full. As if he had pulled something over on his sisters, he would relate the heat of summer (when the berries were ripe), the snakes and bugs, the mosquitoes, and all the other natural horrors of the berry patch but would end his story with fond reminiscences of how sweet the jelly tasted when the snow was on the ground. Especially tasty, he would smugly add, because his sisters picked most of them.

As I recall from my childhood years, the entire family assumed that Mom and Dad met in Alton shortly after he returned from the war, but few had any details and none (to my knowledge) ever bothered to inquire. My sister shed some light on this question: She thought that Mom and Dad met through the "Nixon-Long" connection initiated when Ruby Nixon, Dad's sister, married Bob Long, Pappy's brother. I have a vague memory of Mom mentioning that she, Faye Long, met Dad through Ruby and Bob (maybe one of those family reunion hook-ups) and hence, another 'Nixon-Long' connection. Consequently, Ruby was both Mom's sister-in-law and her aunt; Bob was Mom's brother-in-law and her uncle. My sister continues: Imagine how far we could go with this lineage . . . With no TV, no movies, and no Internet, these reunions and the relationships that they frequently spawned were common in the Midwest at this time.

After much chiding, my sister and I at long last managed to shame Dad into recording his memories of his Mother and Grandmother. It was a masterpiece of guilt that my sister and I wrought. The reasoning that finally worked appealed to his sense of preservation of family history. As we repeatedly told him, and as he ultimately relented, he, and only he, knew any details about his Mother and Grandmother and he owed it to us as family to record them.

We argued that if he did not record these memories, the rest of us would have no memory of them. And it would be his fault. When his guilt finally accumulated to a point where it overtook his fear of writing, he took up pen to relieve himself of the unwanted, worrisome, offspring planted, guilt.

He wrote this narrative well after he finished college, and by the good fortune of his actually dating the manuscript, we know that it was complete for Christmas of 1995. The subject matter, however, reaches back several generations, spanning from approximately 1863 to 1951. His use of direct quotes and conversations reflects the vividness of the memories related to him by his Grandmother and endears her to all of us who are her progeny. Written in two chapters, he titled his reminiscences *Coming to America*. As you read this piece, note the emphasis on the pride of land ownership, its roots in his Grandmother's values, and it's later resurfacing as his personal yardstick of success. Note also the dependence that she felt, again expressed in his later actions, on the use of nature for survival. Finally, notice the sometimes unspoken but clearly discernable strength of family ties, and the individual strength that it must have required to sever their English roots and move to a new and unknown world.

As you read this work, keep two literary items in mind. First, within it there are glimmerings of Dad's ability to uniquely interpret situations and extract humor from them, and then to succinctly express the essence of a situation in a few well chosen, often ironic, and sometimes satirical, thoughts. Second, again note the very strong emphasis on land and property ownership that he internalized from his Mother and Grandmother.

When Dad told the story of the crossing he placed the origin of the Sarginson family in a place called Croule, Lincolnshire, England. When he committed the story to paper, he cited the same place name, spelling it as I have above. I easily found Lincolnshire on the southern coast of England but I could not locate a place called "Croule" despite all my efforts. Even modifying the spelling (Crewell, Crewelle, *etc.*) yielded no positive results. I left it at that.

Early in 2009, while in Hemet, California, I met a man aged some seventy years. He told me that when he was eleven, he and his sister lived in Liverpool in the United Kingdom. Despite compelling stories of the daily bombing and of life in air raid shelters during the German onslaught, the conversation eventually did turn to Lincolnshire. "Sure", he knew of Lincolnshire and had even heard of Croule which he spelled correctly as C-r-e-w-e-l-l. He conspicuously pronounced it as if it were two words - "crew" and "well" -

said quickly with the two "w"s merged into one, and the accent on "crew". His specificity about the pronunciation, bolstered by his insistence on the correct spelling, convinced me that his information was trustworthy. He knew where Crewell was; he had actually been there. Suddenly the location of my father's family was no longer predicated myth but on fact, rooted in geography. Even armed with the exuberance brought by this Brit's fascinating revelations, I still could not find Crewell on a map and continue to believe that it, like Chesterfield, was a small town not sufficiently remarkable to catch the attention of cartographers.

Coming to America

By
MYRON S. NIXON
Christmas 1995

CAPUT PRIMUS

ELEANOR RINGELL SARGINSON: MY GREAT GRANDMOTHER

Croule, Lincolnshire, England
October 6, 1863

William Sarginson sat at his supper table along with his wife Eleanor (Ringell) Sarginson and sipped a last cup of tea. Little Julia, his five year old daughter, sat at the hearth.

Little Julia knew what he would say next and he promptly did. "Eleanor, read the letter again. The one cousin Willie Sarginson sent us from America".

Little Julia immediately picked up her box containing dry grass, tree bark, and wood chips and began to kindle a small fire in the hearth so that it would flame up with more light and allow her mother to see to read better. She had done this many times before.

Eleanor read the letter through and her husband asked her as he always did, "Read the part about the free land again, and the part about the Indians, and the part about the wood and water".

Eleanor read dutifully "The land is free to the immigrant for signing his name on a paper. The Indians are no longer troublesome. They have now moved farther west and now live along the Illinois River. Most of the free land has ample water in the form of springs or small streams. Wood is plentiful in the form of timber. All of this is free for the cutting".

"Now let us count the money again, we must leave as soon as possible" said William. The stones were wriggled out of the base of the hearth and a black leather wallet retrieved from this cavity. The money was counted and William declared it to be very close to enough to pay for passage. The shipping company offered three classes of passage to America: first class, second class and steerage. They would, of course, go by steerage.

Little Julia dreamed that night of being in America, and of all the good things she had heard said of that new country. Little Julia would, some 60 years in the future, be my grandmother.

Grandmother often related to me stories of her passage across the north Atlantic. That was 65 years ago and my memory has undergone many changes since then. I shall try to piece it all together however.

I can't remember where in England they boarded the ship, or what season of the year it was. I would assume they would try to leave in early spring so as to have time to build a cabin on their land before winter.

She told of sailing with the tide one morning and enjoying several days of mild weather.

Then the bad weather caught them. She told of a terrible storm and the wind carrying away a portion of the ship's rigging, of limping into a harbor somewhere in the North Atlantic and staying a long time at a terrible cold place. After repairing the storm damage to the ship the voyage was resumed. Grandmother told of more bad weather, of a baby sister who died and was buried at sea, and of finally reaching New York Harbor. They then passed through Ellis Island and took a train to Chicago. I do not know how William Sarginson, his wife Eleanor, and his daughter Julia made their journey from Chicago south to Chesterfield, Ill., some 300 miles.

Chesterfield is a small town located in southwestern central Illinois. It is about 50 miles south of the state capitol, Springfield, and about 60 miles north of St. Louis.

To the east some 12 miles is Carlinville; to the west are flat agricultural prairies. To the north about ten miles is another small community called Hagærman; to the south some seven miles is Medora. Chesterfield is predominantly a quiet, friendly, Midwestern rural community serving an agricultural populace. The population today, as it has been for some time, is about 300 people.

Most of the small communities, towns, or settlements in this part of Illinois were of ethnic origin. Chesterfield was an English town. Hagærman was an Irish settlement, Carlinville was German, Gillespie was Scottish, and so it went. Mixing was to come later.

William Sarginson now walked more upright, held his head higher, and had more spring in his step. He was a landowner! His land was 40 acres located 3 miles south southeast of the village of Chesterfield. The land was timberland. It was hilly and cut through by two small streams. It had one spring.

He had never before felt so good. It was true that his land was covered with weeds and brush, but that he knew, would soon change, for he was a young man and he would change it himself. And he did. The land, along with the entire country was raw and rough. Life itself was harsh.

In a land with no doctors, no medicine, and no shelter from the elements, life expectancy was low and infant mortality at an all time high. Eleanor Sarginson gave birth to ten children and only four lived to adulthood, Julia, Marshall, Oliver, and Ada.

Julia remained close to the old homestead. Marshall also remained close, married Hannah Burrell and raised 3 children Sidney, Alfred, and Lela. Oliver became a tiler, married Ina Buehlman, and moved to Morrisonville, Ill. As a tiler, his job was to dig and lay tile for drainage on flat crop lands. His children were Myron and Lola. Ada married William Fenton and moved to Decatur, Ill. Her children were William Jr. and Rodna.

Grandma Julia once told of awakening in the night to hear her mother sobbing, then heard her say "William the baby has died". The answer came after a long pause, "Put it at the foot of the bed, we shall bury it come morning". This would seem to be a callous and insensitive answer, but an in depth analysis would see it as merely a reflection of the environment.

Someone once said "Time and tide wait for no man". This is indeed one of the great truths of all time. So the years came and went for William Sarginson. He cut down trees for firewood, grubbed out the stumps and planted his crops. A never ending cycle, the years came and went for Julia also and she became a young lady. Julia became pregnant reputedly by an itinerant wood chopper named Levi Jones, who promptly disappeared, never to be seen again. On May 20, 1890, Julia gave birth to a baby girl. She was named Viola May. This Viola May would one day become my mother.

CAPUT SECUNDUS

VIOLA SARGINSON NIXON: MY MOTHER

Chesterfield, Illinois, USA, May 20, 1890

Little is known of Viola's early childhood life. She always seemed reluctant to discuss it and there was no one else living that I know of who could enlighten us. She did, however, on rare occasions speak of some unusual happenstance in her early life as a child and my two elder sisters and myself are now trying to remember as many as possible of these rare instances.

We do know she lived with her grandparents and they were kind to her. Her mother married a young English immigrant and they moved about a mile east from there.

Albany School was about a mile west of her grandparents' farm and about a mile west of William Sarginson's land. She attended there on an irregular basis. She only attended school during good weather. She had no shoes or overshoes and never went to school during bad weather. She did not attend school often enough to be a member of any regular class. She did, however, learn to read and write along with some skill in mathematics. She once said that she paid close attention to the other classes as they recited, and watched closely when they used the blackboard.

Albany was a one room school house approximately 20 feet wide and 30 feet long. I attended Albany school in the same building my mother attended. My sisters did also. Classes were called to the recitation bench to recite. Then they gave way to the next class to recite.

As Viola describes, the little one room schoolhouses had, in some respects, certain advantages.

At about twelve years she began to work for other people. The more affluent families during that era kept a hired man and a hired girl. The hired man worked outside and the hired girl helped with the housework, washing, scrubbing dishes, caring for the small children, *etc*. They lived with the people they worked for. Viola remained in this type of work until she was about twenty years old. She met a young man about this time and they were married February 4, 1912.

Harley Harrison Nixon was the youngest of eleven children, nine of which lived to adulthood. His parents were George and Mary (Womac) Nixon. George migrated to Girard, Illinois, from Marietta, Ohio, and Mary Womac migrated with her parents from Tennessee to the Carlinville, Illinois, area. Of the eleven children of George and Mary Nixon, there was John, Chas., Albert, Loretta, George, Walter, James, Pearley, and Harley. Two girls died in infancy.

In 1911 Harley Nixon was a student at Blackburn College in Carlinville. His father died at that time and he quit school to go home and manage the farm located about half way between Chesterfield and Carlinville, Illinois, and care for his mother. In 1912, he brought his bride home and they began their life together, he as a farmer and Viola as his bride. The first child to be born to this union was Melba Lucille, born July 12, 1913. The next child born was Ruby Mae, born February 12, 1916.

They had moved since Melba was born and now lived northwest of Carlinville, Illinois, on a farm not far from where they first lived. The next move was to a farm one mile due west of Carlinville, Illinois. The land was level in this entire area of the Illinois Prairie and was black fertile soil. The only drawback was the land was poorly drained and remained wet late in the spring, making it difficult to work because of late planting in the spring. They endured both wet and dry seasons. My mother always said if she had a choice she would prefer the wet season to the dry because during a wet season, they would have pasture for the horses and other livestock. In a dry year they had nothing.

The crops grown here were corn, wheat, oats (soybeans didn't come until 1940). Hay crops were alfalfa, clover, and timothy (timothy was forage for horses). Portions of these crops were marketed. Also portions were fed to livestock and horses.

So they endured both good and bad times. But they were happy and rejoiced that they were together and had their family around them. There was even more rejoicing when, on November 25, 1919, their third child was born, this time a boy and was promptly christened Myron Stanley. Their rejoicing, however, was short lived. In February of 1920 Harley came down with the flu and on February 14 succumbed to pneumonia and died. He is buried at Charity Church about 4 miles northwest of Carlinville, Illinois.

This left Viola with Melba 6 years old, Ruby 3, and Myron 10 weeks old. She knew her duty and immediately set about executing it. She had a sale and sold the horses and other livestock, along with the farm machinery. She then bought a small house in Carlinville, Illinois, and moved there along with her three children.

At the time of Harley's death, Clara came to stay with us. She came to help Viola with her work and to help care for the small children. Clara was the eldest child of John and Bessie Nixon. John was Harley's oldest brother and lived a short distance away. I understand Clara came as a temporary helper but she never returned to her own family.

My mother tried to support us by washing and ironing clothes for other people, but it soon became apparent that this would not work.

In the meantime, John Nixon rented a farm known as the "Hunter Farm" about six miles west of Carlinville, Illinois. This farm was generally flat ground but had a small brook running through it. It was surrounded by other farms. It took approximately an hour and a half to go to town. I don't remember going more than once or twice. Our only transportation was by horse and buggy.

This farm had two houses on it, and he offered one of the houses to my mother. She readily accepted. Now she was back on her own element and she started raising chickens. Each spring she hatched about one hundred white Leghorn chickens. She kept the pullets for laying hens and we ate the roosters. We also had a large garden with a large strawberry patch. Everywhere we lived we always had a large garden. We planted and cultivated it ourselves. Nothing was wasted. It was my mother's answer to putting food on our table. I always tell people to this day that I was raised primarily on potatoes, beans, blackberries, and Vicks VapoRub.

We also roamed the countryside picking wild blackberries and dewberries. She would never quit until we had a hundred quarts in the cellar. We also gathered large quantities of nuts each fall, hickory, black walnuts, and hazelnuts. My mother did all of the canning. My favorite canned food was blackberries. We stored canned goods and root crops in the cellar. Nuts were stored on the floor of upstairs bedrooms. We all had chores to do at each end of the day, carrying water and feed, garden work, *etc.*

We also had a wide array of pets at different times. We had cats, dogs, baby squirrels, raccoons, crows, *etc.* I started hunting and trapping before I was 10 years old. Hunting ginseng and golden seal (yellow root) about this time also occupied some of my time. My mother encouraged me in these activities for sometimes I made money at it.

We were happy and we were successful but of course it didn't last. John Nixon failed to rent the farm. I don't know why the landowner refused to rent but the landowner may, for any reason, or for no reason, refuse to rent the land to the existing tenant, poor crops being the most common reason for not renewing the lease. We were obligated to move. My mother, as a last resort, decided to move in with Grandma, her mother, who lived about five miles to the south and west of our present location.

We then attended Albany School, located four miles south of Chesterfield, Illinois. We were now two and a half miles from school so we had a five mile walk every day. Things didn't seem to go well there. The reasons we didn't stay here longer were that we were much too far from school and too far from town. The following year we moved into Chesterfield, Illinois. My mother rented a small brick house close to the school. I was now in the fourth grade, Melba was in high school, and Ruby was now staying with Mr. & Mrs. Chas. Jones. Ruby wanted to stay with the Jones family and finish her grade school education because these old people [asked] her to stay, even paid her a small amount to do so. This was not unusual at this time. Poor people with several children often did this. She attended Albany School in the seventh grade.

At about this point in time, early nineteen thirty, Clara began to work as a telephone switchboard operator and later my mother also began as an operator. My mother worked at night from 9:00 P. M. until 7:00 A. M. This sounds ridiculous I know but it is true. The Great Depression was well on its way by then, and jobs were almost impossible to find.

At about this time I think my mother could see a faint dim light at the end of the tunnel. Some years before she had set her goal to raise us up until we were old enough to fend for ourselves. She had taught us all to work, to know right from wrong. She had educated us and saw to our needs as we went along. Melba was through high school and now had a job in house work. Ruby was still in high school and had become quite adept at setting hair for others. She kept quite busy at this.

My mother had one more move to make and about 1931 we moved from the little brick house east about a block and a half to a large white house owned by Chas. Wilton. Clara was still working as a telephone operator along with my mother who still worked there at night. Ruby and me were in high school. We would graduate in 1934 and 1937.

The Great Depression was still on. One elderly gentleman who had weathered the depression in Missouri told me he made oak and hickory axe handles for a living. On one occasion he had bought a sack of beans, paid for them with axe handles, and received two hammer handles in change. Along about 1938 he said he knew times were getting better, for he had seen a rabbit cross the road and only three people were chasing it.

As the mid thirties came and went, my mother and Clara continued to work at the telephone office. Ruby married Olin Long and moved to Alton, Illinois. Melba married Clyde Phelps and moved to the country. In 1939 I became employed at the Alton Box Board paper factory in Alton, Illinois.

About this time Hitler invaded Poland and the war clouds were gathering. It became clear that we would soon be embroiled in the European war. All the politicians talked against it, but I think secretly they worked in favor of it.

I joined the Army and left home November 25 (my birthday) in 1941. December 7th, the Japanese bombed Pearl Harbor and I knew I was in for the duration of the war. This was probably the hardest single blow my mother had suffered since my father's death.

I came home in June 1945 at the end of the war. My sisters both lived in Alton then. Melba's children were Jerry, Martha, and Margie. Ruby's children were Keith, Terry, and Kaye. I was married to Faye Long on May 31, 1946. My children are Joseph and Gale.

My mother retained reasonably good health until early 1951 when she was stricken by colon cancer and passed away in April 1951. She died knowing she had completed her long task of raising three children, a task that she had never abandoned or wavered from. She is buried beside my father at Charity Baptist Cemetery about three miles northwest of Carlinville, Illinois.

III. WAR STORIES (1941-1945)

Assembling and sorting Dad's works, I ended up with several papers related to his war time experiences that did not fit well into any other time frame. The ultimate decision was to place them at the closest chronological point in his life (A or B . . .). So they are here, between the ancestral, earlier look at *Family Origins* and stories of his later life following discharge from the military, or from about November 5, 1941 to June 1945. These four pieces are some of the stories from his war days that he ultimately decided to tell. They contain very little information about the conflict itself, or about his attitude toward the Army, but they focus on events that were important to, and had an effect on, him. Perhaps in a larger sense, they also reflect how the war experience affected those from his generation that survived.

We know that Dad was in the Army for about three and a half years. After about a year (I assume in basic training and AIT - Advanced Individual Training), the military briefly assigned him to Australia and New Zealand, ultimately landing in the Fijii Islands (1943-1944?). His assignment there was to live in the jungles among the natives to better learn how to conduct commando type military operations. Becoming a jungle commando must have been quite a culture shock for a boy raised on the farm in central Illinois.

Much later, while he was in college, he tapped into these memories as a springboard to prepare some of his class assignments. Two of these survive. The first appears to have been a research assignment to select a geographic area, research it in the library, and prepare a report on the people of that region and their origins. He selected Melanesia. His paper, which he titled *Origin of Fijii Islanders*, he did not date but in context with the second piece described below, I estimated it was prepared sometime in 1974 in an Anthropology class. He clearly is the author of this somewhat fragmentary report style work. There is no temporal setting for the work that spans the origins of the Fijii peoples until the present.

The companion piece is not titled but he dated it March 11, 1974. Again it appears to have been an Anthropology assignment. He was the author and the setting of the work was *ca*. 1943-1944. It is a combination of prose and reporting and surprisingly shows fairly good observational skills as a field anthropologist, a sleeping ambition roused by his time in the islands - but not yet fully awakened.

When in the Fijii Islands, he learned the local language, observed native customs and rituals, plotted out the typical day of an Islander, speculated on the Fijii peoples' origins, participated in rituals, drew conclusions, and, amid it all, apparently enjoyed working with the people of Fijii. In this work he is the amateur anthropological observer recording details and reporting them (albeit years later) through his writings. His teacher gave no grade for the work but commented that it was a good report but needed to be "revisited and rewritten". The requested rework and submission was not among the papers that I have.

In the next work, *The Left Handed Cannibal*, he transcends from anthropological observer to participant observer - he actually was part of the story he relates. This prose style essay dated July 31, 1997, tells of his experiences around 1943-44. He relates an interesting story about Fijii hunters on a quest for turtles. This does not appear to be a class assignment, rather this is his own written account of one of his favorite stories about his life with the people of Fijii.

While in Fijii, he picked up a number of things: a language, firsthand experience as an anthropologist, military training, commando tactics(?), and malaria. He did occasionally speak about this ailment and related spending nearly a year in state side hospitals in an attempt to recover. He once told me about the first stages of recovering from malaria while still in the islands. He was in a tent and there was a monkey climbing around the rafters above his bed – perhaps he was hallucinating - or maybe there really was a monkey. From some of his confused memories, I can only conclude that he spent most of this year on medications that altered his consciousness. As a person who neither smoke nor drank, these medications were very difficult for him to tolerate and he often reacted unpredictably.

In later life, the malaria attacks were fewer but when he went into the hospital for any kind of treatment that required anesthesia or other mind-modifying medications, he seemed to "flash back" to the period of malaria delirium. At one point he went to the hospital for quadruple bypass surgery. Before the doctors operated, I warned them of this potential side effect. They finished their work and moved him into the recovery room. In the middle of the night, they noted he was gone. They found him in the parking lot, attempting to, in his words, "escape". I believed then and I still do that his escape from the hospital despite his physical condition was stimulated by one of his flashbacks to the malaria wards and the medications that he had been given. Astonished, and finally retrieving him from the parking lot, they took what I said more seriously.

The final piece in this section he dated August 10, 1989. For him it is an unusual 'poetic' piece written partially under the influence of drugs in the middle of a sleepless night. By reading *At the Clinic/At the Hospital* you can see firsthand the horror and paranoia he experienced in these drug induced states, even though his sense of humor shows through as usual.

Subject: Origin of Fijii Islanders (College years 1973-1980)

From Profiles in Ethnology by Elman R. Service, Page 230

People of Melanesia are of three racial strains in varying degrees of mixture. The first arrivals were probably short statured Negroes, called Negritos form the direction of Malaysia. Next came lighter skinned group called variously Proto Caucasoid, Archaic White, Ainoid, and Veddoid. The third group came much later called the Melanesians.

A mixture of the above peoples were often captured by European ships and sold as slaves in the cotton plantations of Fijii and sugar plantations in Australia.

Excerpts from Habitat, Economy & Society by Daryll Forde, Page 176

While the Samoans and Tahitians were recognized by eighteenth century voyagers as being almost European in appearance the Fijians were more like Melanesians.

Handbook of the Colony Leonard G. Usher, Page 17

"Some fragmentary stories tell of arrival in canoes of the progenitors of the race, driven by gales from somewhere to the west of Fiji".

Few Fijians can trace their descent beyond ten generations, they then tend to drift off into myth and superstition (my own research).

The Living Races of Man by Carleton Coon, Page 171

Since W.W.II a number of archaeologists working in Melanesia, Micronesia and Polynesia have turned up useful information on stratified sites. The oldest date so far recorded from Melanesia is 847 B. C. at a site in New Caledonia. One sample or reading from Viti Levu in Fijii gives 46 B. C. as the time when the island was first settled.

[Instr: Grade = C+]

Anthropology of the Fijii Islanders: Mar. 11, 1974

MYRON NIXON

Nov. 1941 war was imminent. I joined the Army and asked to be put into a fighting outfit. My wish was promptly granted. After a quick look around I became aware of my mistake. Such inefficiency, ineptness and stupidity was unbelievable. So I decided to make the most of it, fight the war and get out as soon as possible. I also decided to decline any advance in rank, not wishing to be a part of such a farce.

In July, 1942, after a brief stay in New Zealand and Australia, I found myself in the Fiji Islands. Being very much interested in the flora and fauna of the tropics, I bought books and pamphlets and began to study the language. In order to gain further knowledge I soon realized I must study the people also, which I did. The British had two Batallions of Native troops in training on the Island, along with a Native Commando school back in the jungle. Some Americans were also selected for this training and I was nominated because of my ability to speak the Native language.

I spoke little or no English for three months, and I must admit I seldom knew what the hell was going on. My hat is off to any and all anthropologists who go and live with primitive peoples for any length of time. The dirt, the bedbugs, lice, stench and uncertainty is something one must see to believe.

Fiji.

Location: S. Pacific, Lats 15 degrees, 42 minutes and 21 degrees 02 South and between Long. 178 degrees 12 minutes West and 176 degrees, 53 minutes East. Midway between Kingdom of Tonga and the French Colony of New Caledonia.

Comprised of 250 islands, about 80 inhabited. Rugged - mountainous - densely timbered - volcanic. Fringed by coral reefs and lagoons. Prevailing winds E to SE. Many rivers and streams.

Capital city Suna, located on largest island, Viti Levu.

Languages - hundreds of dialects, several on each island. The language I learned was known as the "bou" language and was being currently taught in the schools. When I was present most people tried to stay somewhere near the bou language, however, only the children had a good working knowledge of it. Once I hired a Chinese boy as interpreter. He claimed to have learned English while mooching in the streets of Suna. He knew only a few words of English however, and I had to let him go. His vocabulary consisted of "good-a-fella" and "somma-bich". This was the only place I ever encountered where a man could, in essence, name himself, by his generosity, or lack of it.

A typical day in the life of a Fiji Islander:

Arise when he felt like it.
Work in his garden an hour, if he wished.
Eat everything left over from the day before.
Rest in the shade

Play with the children.
Visit neighbors.
Repair fishing gear. Sharpen machete. Take a siesta.
Whole village go to river or beach.
Men catch fish for supper.
Women wash all clothing.
Return to village and eat evening meal.
Rest in the shade.
Take short nap.
Prepare for bull session.
Tell stories until most everyone falls asleep

It was the story telling session each night that intrigued me most. Even when I understood only portions of it, my interest never waned, for they had a way of acting out a story, and after all the audience became involved. No wonder they were tired all the next day. The stories always dealt with the past, of war, cannibalism, sexual prowess and great potency. Of the occult, great mysticism and superstition. I once asked an old man [said to be a recovering cannibal] what piece of human flesh he liked best. He held his left arm aloft and pointed to his forearm, and described it as sweet meat, and very tender, and the two bones (radius and ulna) made excellent drum sticks later. He insisted the left arm was best to eat, because the right one was much tougher (most people are naturally right handed). Some time later when an outrigger canoe capsized and left me on the high seas with three native boys one whole day and one night, I couldn't get this out of my mind. With my luck, I'll bet all three of them were left-handed.

I noticed no homosexuality, no sexual deviation, no problem with children, no sadistic traits. I was astonished one evening to hear a boy of 15 asked his mother to instruct his sister of 14 to wash his clothes the next day, because his sister was sitting beside him at the time. I learned later that siblings after they reach the ages of twelve are not allowed to converse with each other, or sleep in the same house. This is a built in rule to control incest, I suppose.

I witnessed no marriages, no puberty rites, and very few special events of any kind. These people live very close and in nearly absolute harmony with nature. They practiced no self mutilation, body scarification or tattooing.

People

People of Fiji

Melanesian predominantly, however some islands east of Viti Levu show some evidence of Polynesian influence. They ignore the other population and seldom inter breed with the Chinese, E. Indians, Taugau or Samoan people. They are large structured people. The average male being over six feet tall and in excess of two hundred pounds. Good athletes, excellent swimmers. Color is shiny black to dull brown, hair kinky, eyes dark, thick lips, flat faces, lacking the sloping forehead, generally. Happy people, always singing, very generous with food and extremely peaceful. Good sense of humor.

I was extremely surprised when years later I heard a broadcast from the Belgian Congo and I seemed to understand portions of the language. A political figure there named Patrice Lumumba was speaking. In Fijiian, "B" is always pronounced as if it had an "M" before it. Now consider the name "Lububa". Pronounce it and out comes Lumumba. Also the oft mispronounced "TABU". "A" is always short "a", so now we have a pronunciation of "TAMBU". It is my opinion the Fijian people come from the same stock as the Congolese. I suppose Anthropologist have connected them before, but I have never read or heard of it. Several other words seem to be similar also, and the chant or rhythm with which they deliver their speech seems similar.

[Instr: Grade = none. Comments: Report is good as a beginning. Why not research some of the questions you've been asking yourself (e. g. people's

26

origin, reason for rules, etc.)? Add the answer and resubmit. It's an excellent beginning but it seems a bit quick and superficial for someone of your intelligence and broad interests. Please don't be offended - I mean this in the most positive sense].

The Left Handed Cannibal (Written July 31, 1997; setting 1942-1943?)

by Myron S. Nixon

During World War II, I was a soldier in the Army Infantry. In due time I was sent to the Fijii Islands, to fortify the islands in case the Japanese landed there. Some months later the powers that be decided that some of us should learn how to survive in the jungle and undergo commando training also.

The British had mobilized two battalions of native troops and kept them back in the interior of "Viti Levu" (Big Island). I was sent to live with a small group of these native soldiers.

In the evenings we often went to a native village and visited with the villagers and we did what, I suppose, grown men do everywhere, we sat around and told lies.

One evening the subject matter got around to cannibalism and an elderly gray haired man told about his experiences some 50 years before. He talked to great length and when he had finished, I asked him a question that had all along intrigued me: "What piece did you like the best?"

I had made up my mind that if he hesitated before answering he would probably be making it up. He never hesitated at all, just held his forearm up, and gently stroked it, all the time explaining that it was his favorite piece. Knowing that everyone has a favorite piece of chicken or beef, etc. he was probably telling the truth. He went on to explain that a right handed man would have a tough right arm because he used it more, and it was best to eat his left arm. A left handed man, it was best to eat his right arm, for the same reason.

A few days later some of my fellow soldiers were going over to another island to catch some salt-water turtles. I decided to accompany them. We were to leave by outrigger canoe early the next morning. We met on the beach before sunrise and I scarcely got sat down when they asked me if I was right or left handed!

Two thoughts banged through my head: why am I here? And what's for supper around here?

I soon realized they were not casing me up for lunch, but were merely asking which side of the canoe I would like to paddle from. Everyone was expected to help row the boat until clear of the ground swell.

I suppose the moral of this story might be: "Never trust a left handed cannibal."

At the Clinic & At The Hospital: The Poetry of Myron (August 10, 1989)

Dear Joe and Colleen:

One night while I was at the hospital I just couldn't fall asleep. Deciding to sit up and write someone a letter, the thought came to me that I should make note of the things that had happened to me the past several days. This prose poured out of me so long and fast that I decided to write it all down.

Later when I went home I could never find this stuff I had written that night. I was deeply concerned that I had left all of it at the hospital. If those nurses and the doctor found it I knew I was cooked. They would surely give me a strychnine sandwich and a glass of prestone if I ever returned. I vowed never to return!

Later I found it all and breathed much easier.

Now I am leaving it up to you two to edit the whole thing, put the verses into proper order and correct mistakes, etc.

Happy editing!

Love
Dad

AT THE CLINIC

The doctor turned to the nurse
and I heard what he said
This guy's really shaky
He'll probably drop dead.

If he drops dead at the door
turn his feet half about
like he was just coming in
and not going out.

AT THE HOSPITAL

The doctor frowned darkly
the nurse stood aghast
that gave me the feeling
I was breathing my last.

The doctor said mister
you've had it and how
could you just sign this paper?
and please pay me now.

Nothing works any more
I'm falling apart
can't see anything
can't hear myself fart.

With a fast beating pulse
and a run away heart
I knew I was a goner
right from the start.

Life changes completely
they say at my age
nothing works anymore
Guess I should turn the page.

Can't see any more
I'm falling apart

Joseph M. Nixon

my hands are arthritic
can't hear myself fart.

Prune juice and fiber
jogging and all
may keep me a-going
till this coming fall.

I asked my physician
please define my position
A prognosis long overdue.
So come on old chap
just cut out the crap
and tell me for sure if I'm through.

As I told you before
you're a goner for sure.
I doubt that you'll last out the night.
So swallow your pill
and make out your will
I'll be glad when you're out of my sight.

My sisters came in
they looked pretty grim
said "I doubt you'll ever recover
you look pretty sad
but not quite so bad
if you keep your head under the cover".

The doc came back in
his face long and thin
said "you're looking worse somehow
I give you fair warning
you'll be a crappie by morning
Could you please pay your bill now?"

My sisters came in again
they looked pretty grim
They really were singing the blues.
"It's hopeless dear brother
you'll never recover

Sure glad we're not in your shoes".

Then came the head nurse
wide as a hearse
she shouted from outside the door
She said she couldn't come in
she was not quite that thin
and her butt wouldn't pass thru the door.
One thing I can't stand
is that awful old bedpan
sitting there is such a disgrace
The nurse said "It's quite necessary
you'd best not be contrary
for you're looking quite full in the face".

I think I should mention
how they got my attention
It was like a big game of tag.
While I watched the TV
they slipped up behind me
and snipped off a slice of my bag.

To my right down two aisles
are the ones with the piles
It's a down right shame what they do
They catch them unawares
in those cane bottom chairs
and snip off everything that falls through.

The in came the head nurse
she was as wide as a hearse
said she had heard an uproar
said she wouldn't be back
and it was a fact
her behind would not pass through the door.

One old man told me
"Just kindly behold me"
then his head began to jerk and to wag
"While I watched TV
they slipped up behind me

and snipped off a slice of my bag".

My sisters cam in
after things had calmed
said I looked as if
I was already embalmed.

"You may last until morning
But I can't see how
Better make out your will
and please pay me now".

You look awful sad
I doubt you'll recover
you look best of all
with your head under the cover.

Ol boy you've had it
you'll never get well
with one foot in this place
and the other in hell.

These three verses are in reference to Toot. She now is <u>35</u> instead of forty.

I gulp down my fiber
Jog often and fast
with a cholesterol meter
firm in my grasp.

Now this new math perplexes me
twenty and twenty they say
don't still add up to forty
like it did in my day.

Always before,
since I've been alive
twenty and twenty was forty
now its only thirty five.

IV. THIS LAND IS MY LAND (1949-1950)

According to my parents, we lived in Alton, Illinois, before we moved to Chesterfield. I have no memory of that and so have always taken their account as true. My sister and I learned further that when we moved to Chesterfield, Mom and Dad operated the local restaurant on the east side of the square in town. In my most recent visits to Chesterfield, there still was a restaurant there, perhaps now best described as a tavern that I think also serves burgers.

Although I don't know for sure, I suspect Mom and Dad didn't own the establishment, but they staffed and ran it on someone else's payroll. Who that might have been I never knew. While I can easily picture Mom in the kitchen flipping burgers and making fries, it is nearly inconceivable to me that Dad would have been the counter man. It required too much face time for him to be comfortable; it was not in his character to tolerate others in the volume that job would require. To envision this account of their early lives together, I have even tried to picture them in the opposite roles. But I could not imagine Dad being content in the kitchen with the burgers. Mom, on the other hand, would have been a natural at the counter interacting with the public for unlike Dad, she thrived on face time. Whatever the details, this arrangement did not last long despite what I am sure were their absolute best efforts at trying to make it work.

Some of my first memories are of a house owned by Velma Davis situated in the western Chesterfield suburbs, near what was and still may be the most lucrative enterprise in town: the grain elevator. I suppose I was a little over two years old and my sister, if she were born at the time, would have been an infant. I was not yet in school and was still fully in possession of that sweet, unstained, natural innocence commonly associated with childhood. Cynicism and I had not yet met.

I made my first friend there. His name was Ross. If life were a yardstick, I was still between the one and two inch markers and Ross was struggling not to fall off the other end. Chesterfield at the time was a small town, totaling possibly 300 people. If it ever had a homeless person, it was old Ross, my friend.

I remember him living in a one room house (a trailer?) a few doors down the street from us. Regardless of the weather, he wore a wool coat year round and he walked with a limp. One of those heavy, black, long, coats with big shiny black buttons with anchors stamped on them that remind you of a Sherlock Holmes movie. Life had not been good to Ross. Only in retrospect can I imagine the disappointments, the unfulfilled dreams, the loves gone sour, the ambitions crushed, the lost dogs, that he might have held in his memory and which, sadly, had brought him to his station as Chesterfield's only homeless person.

Since I was born late in 1946 and I was about two years old when I befriended Ross, the year must have been about 1948-1949. As a child I was dimly aware of a cycle of good and evil in the world. Everyone talked about the Great Depression as such a "bad" thing and then about its end as such a "good" thing. Then came WWII – a bad thing - and then its end – a good thing. But that year evil was again afoot. That coke-bottle-horn-rimmed-glasses-wearing, white coated, egghead scientist, Jonas Salk, had not yet figured out how to attenuate the virus that caused it, so polio was on everyone's mind – a bad thing.

That really didn't concern me nor did it seem to bother Ross who would just square up the collar of his wool coat against the summer heat as if nothing had happened. In my immature years I befriended him and he returned the kindness for his own reasons. He probably saw me as harmless and possibly amusing; maybe I finally was a ray of hope for him; after all, he didn't have a dog. I'll never know.

My parents did not discourage this friendship. And, not worried about roving Chesterfield street gangs kidnapping me for ransom, they essentially let me run free within a reasonable distance of the (Velma Davis) house. With this latitude, Ross and I spent a lot of time together, I assume talking, throwing rocks, petting dogs, and other pastimes that would amuse the very young and the very old alike.

As time passed, I slowly developed a limp, not a serious defect, but noticeable. Mom and Dad panicked because of the currently uncontrollable polio scare - a bad thing. They became increasingly convinced that I had contracted the dreaded disease and would be a lifelong cripple. There were medical appointments; they found nothing. They talked to the preacher; also nothing. They read books and they listened to the radio every time the station broadcast something remotely addressing polio; they learned lots of information on new cases and the spread of the disease across the land, but they found little help for them and their afflicted boy. They read the paper dutifully and sorrowfully noted diagnosed cases as close as the next town. As if to fuel their already immolated fears, I showed no change. I am sure that they had endless conversations between themselves about what to do about me and about how to protect my sister (born or unborn) from this walking plague known as her older brother, but nothing was really done and still I showed no signs of change.

I do not know exactly how this happened, but I imagine Dad sitting on the porch one evening as Ross and I walked by when a thought occurred to him. Later, enticing me into some invented game in the yard, he saw me running normally and confirmed his suspicions: polio had not infected me after all, I was simply was mimicking Ross's limp. A good thing.

Being just one of many childhood stages, it passed as quickly as it had developed. Mom and Dad now could turn their undivided attention to whatever the next bad thing might be but I was OK; and they didn't have to worry about my sister anymore; and they didn't have to fear having more crippled, maimed, deformed, or polio infected children; and the world as mirrored on the gangless streets of Chesterfield was back in good order. I don't know what ever happened to Ross but if there's a place in heaven for dogless homeless people in wool coats, I'm sure he is in it. Were Mom and Dad still alive, I doubt that they would share my kind thoughts for my old, limping, friend.

From there we moved to the Middlecoff place. I never met anyone named Middlecoff and am sure of his existence only by virtue of the namesake real estate which we came to occupy. A farmhouse, the Middlecoff property occupied a rural context about four miles east of Chesterfield. Corn and bean fields surrounded it, rotated in their agricultural rhythm.

Access to the property was *via* Illinois State Highway 111 leaving Chesterfield heading east-northeast. That route would take you past the City Cemetery on your right. Taking the first exit to the right at a point where the paved road (SR-111) turns 90 degrees to the north, the road to the Middlecoff place strikes straight east. Following this rural road approximately two miles, you would encounter a dirt road striking to the right at a 90 degree angle. Taking it south through the fields would take you past a pond on the left (east) to an unimproved, dirt, intersection. In a quarter of a mile the road to the right would put you at the Middlecoff place. I have not revisited this place in my adult life and do not know whether it still stands or not.

As a young child I have only a vague memory of this part of life, but I recall living among the corn and bean fields in rural Illinois. I do vividly remember terribly cold winters when Dad would scrounge for wood both to heat the place and to cook in the archaic wood stove over which Mom dutifully prepared meals. She never complained about that old stove, the marginally dependable heating system, the absolute isolation, or any of the other everyday irritations. Looking back I wonder if the still fresh memories of a small house in Alton combined with a large family and five sisters in a bed, made the sheer space of an entire house for four people (two of which were small) seem like an extravagance that easily erased other hardships, like the stove or the heater.

I remember many cold nights and snowed in days at that place which, in the winter, was neither accessible from the outside nor escapable from the inside. In the summer, I remember climbing on a rickety old shed on the right side of and in front of the farmhouse, searching a ramshackle garage of sorts directly across the dirt driveway, exploring and climbing in various barns and silos, and playing up and down the country lane leading by the edge of the corn field up to the house. I also remember going out to the end of the lane to catch a ride with Joyce VanPelt in her station wagon to go to school. Since I began school at age four, this must have been in about 1950.

At about that time, Dad bought a Jeep, not one of the modern ones with electronic enhancements, catalytic converters, roll bars, sport detailing, and other Eddie Bauer accessories. No, this was a real military "surplus property" Jeep. It had two seats, no top, a manual three speed transmission, and full time involuntary four wheel drive. Only the Jerry can and the spare tire were missing, both undoubtedly "borrowed" somewhere along whatever supply stream Dad had plucked this prize from. The four wheel drive permitted access to and from the house when other vehicles would not navigate the snowy or muddy traverse.

Built for generic military service and ease of operation, that Jeep's only security feature was a single key ignition switch. One day Dad could not find that key. I remember that we searched for hours inside the house, in the grass along the access lane, in the mail box, in pants and jacket pockets, anywhere conceivable that might have secreted the elusive key. We did eventually find it but the unhappy lost key episode cemented the memory of that vehicle indelibly in my mind from that point forward.

Dad apparently rented the Middlecoff place for he did no repairs to it other than those necessary to make it warmer in the winter and routine maintenance such as replacing broken windows and torn screens. We did not stay in this house long; although vague, it seems to me to have been about a year.

While in temporary residence at the Middlecoff place, Mom and Dad made a couple of decisions what would change their lives - and those of my sister (now born) and me. First, in an effort to restructure his life after the military intervention, Dad applied for and accepted a position with the Post Office. He would become the rural mail delivery person for Chesterfield. That phrase – rain, snow, sleet, or hail . . . will not delay the mail – became a reality and that Jeep which I now thoroughly detested was a godsend when those very conditions prevailed to confound his appointed rounds.

Second, and no doubt partially predicated on the steady income that would now be forthcoming, they bought a house. It was located in western Chesterfield, not far from (north of) the Velma Davis place. With this purchase they became free to do as they pleased on their own property, free to fix things, to plant things, and to grow fruits, nuts, and children. No longer were there rules imposed by an absentee owner, no one to tell them how to do things. Finally, they could say with absolute ownership: "This land is my land".

Grandmother would have been proud, indeed, for her grandson and his wife had become successful in the very land that was her dream before them. It was Dad's turn to ". . . walk more upright, to hold his head higher, and to feel a spring in his step" just like the father he never knew. Now they had a place of their own. And my sister and I would no longer have to be Children of the Corn.

As the local mail carrier, Dad had two rural routes initially and, if the weather was good, he would drive his Jeep around them in the course of a day. In fairly short order, he rerouted the delivery circuit to reduce the necessary time to about 5 hours per day (albeit six days a week). By beginning early in the morning, he could finish by 12:30 or 1:00 in the afternoon. This left him with half a day every day to spend as he wished. He worked various jobs in addition to the post office – digging graves, making wooden road/address markers for the local cemeteries, raising cattle, helping the neighbors put up hay, and various other small jobs and soon paid off the note on his newly acquired property.

Once in residence, he immediately and happily threw himself at planting and caring for the botanical menagerie that either he had already or he soon would plant: mulberries, nut trees, blackberries, gooseberries, horseradish, flowering shrubs, *etc.* In keeping with the lessons learned from his Grandmother and his Mother, the plants that bore edible foodstuffs were his primary passion. He tended them, pruned them, and eventually developed them into several different hybrid varieties, some unique in the plant world.

Once on the family homestead in the western suburbs of Chesterfield, Dad began to fix everything, for this house and the land that surrounded it were his. We crawled under the house to fix plumbing, tore out floors and replaced them with fine hardwood, added heating vents, replaced the ceiling, bought new appliances, cleaned out the cellar, cleared brush, remodeled the kitchen, added new windows, and – significantly – began to plant trees and landscape the grounds. He planted pecans, walnuts, hickories, hazelnuts – all the trees that would ultimately bear the fruit and nuts that were so important to him as a child. Although necessity no longer demanded it, Dad was making us self sufficient and doing it on his own terms.

Illinois is not a dry place, not a desert by any means. But, as any local farmer will tell you in clear and unmistakable terms, the supply of rain water is irregular. To solve this problem, Dad decided to take matters into his own hands. Chesterfield had no municipal water system to tap into so Dad surveyed his land, isolated a particular hollow just behind (west of) the house, dammed up one end, and created his own water source – a pond. Before it filled (recall the irregular rainfall), he also ran piping from the pond to the house and other locations around the property where he thought a water source would be useful.

Once complete and functional, it worked marvelously – for a few weeks. Then, in the summer, when the warm weather and the sunlit conditions were just right, the newly arrived algae responded by gracing the water and its surface with a green coating of slime. OK. Dad got some ducks who got real fat but who couldn't keep up and the slime was getting into and clogging all of his meticulously excavated and buried water pipes.

The Farm Bureau guy said he needed to install a filter to clean the water before it entered his system and thereby keep out the clogging debris. Oh yeah, and the filter had to be underwater or the system would "suck air". Now comes a masterpiece of Dad's engineering. Not wanting to buy a filtration system, he managed to get his hands on an old metal milk can. Holding about 4-5 gallons, each milk can was steel(?) with a pop off lid about 8" across. He bored a hole in the bottom of the can and installed a fitting to allow water to flow in and out of the can which he filled with charcoal (yes, the kind you still buy for an outdoor grill), and the lid he punctured and fitted similar to the bottom. Replacing the cover and then adding an anchor, he positioned the entire device such that the lid was directly below the water surface. A boat, he reckoned, could provide easy access to change it. Suffice to say that over the years, swimming out to change Bud's filter became something of a rite of passage for every macho teen age boy in town.

But he had a pond, a filter, a watering system, so what was missing? With two kids already walking and not yet swimming, it became obvious to him that he need a dock. This would become one of his stock stories and my sister tells it well. As she recently related: The sisters, Wimp, Bernice, and Ruthie (Thelma was in Florida), gathered their husbands, and they all came to Chesterfield one Sunday to "help" Dad build the dock. Keep in mind that none of these men had ever hammered a nail, so you can imagine the fun Dad had with this. Armed with hammers, nails, tool belts, and determination, they proceeded to build. I'm guessing that Dad also filled their tool belts with rocks. Immediately Laverne (Bernice's husband) fell in the pond, followed by Chod (Wimp's) and Eddie (Ruthie's). She continues: As I understand it, they accomplished little building but a lot of cursing and laughing occurred. Mom, Ruthie, and Bernice, being the ever-sympathetic wives, ran to the house for the camera. I might still have these pictures.

My Sister continues: Once the dock was completed, Dad proclaimed that you and I had to pass two tests before he would allow us to swim without life jackets. The first requirement was that we had to be able to swim around the newly completed dock two times without stopping. The second was that we had to swim nonstop to the filter (yes, by then it was a landmark) and back. No problem for us; we quickly met the challenges and were each rewarded with new fins. AND no more life jackets!! This, of course, to the consternation of visiting fisherman who had to deal with our constant diving, yelling, and splashing while they were fishing.

Fixing up the property was a very busy time for all of us and this was not a time when Dad had many opportunities to write, nor did he have any inclination to do so. We all focused on making the new home more comfortable and livable. As a consequence, he neither produced nor can I include any of his written works from the time when he was making a transition from an itinerant worker to a full time government employee who also owned his own land and home. While free of literary production, it was a period of both physical and mental opportunities for him; a period which saw growth in both dimensions. And, as he told it, when he taught his kids to swim.

V. WHY PLANT THAT TREE, GRANDMA? (1950-1963)

We always stored food for the winter in the cellar. Each day Grandma would say you can go into the cellar and eat the one apple with a bad spot on it. That way, we could eat bad apples all winter! (Myron S. Nixon).

Very shortly after we moved into the house in Chesterfield, Dad began to improve his new home and his land. To his thinking, the land was a clean slate with only a few suffering and ignored plants: some irritating (to barefoot children) evergreen trees at the street end of the driveway, a pair of weary, neglected elms on either side of the front walk, and a huge oak tree sorely in need of attention. The first step was to remove the terminally effected plants and to tend to the struggling oak. Then his attention turned to cultivation and nurturing of the land and its herbal tenants.

In the pasture about a quarter mile northeast of the house was a mature wild mulberry tree, a treasure in Dad's mind. In the fall he harvested the fruit, savoring each wild berry. Soon, though, he realized that there were other mulberries with different and sometimes more pleasing characteristics. Some were larger, some more tasty, some had bigger berries, some tasted sweeter, some bore earlier, some were more attractive to wildlife, *etc*. He learned that you did not have to plant a new tree and wait for the bearing years. Instead, you could trim an especially good tree in the neighbor's yard that bore good berries and graft the cuttings (its scions) onto other trees, often located closer to home. Rather than waiting for a sapling to reach maturity and then to bear fruit, within a couple of years you could harvest berries from the scions that contained your favorite characteristics right from your own yard. Soon every mulberry tree in the pasture, and, more often than not, in the neighbors' pastures, was thus grafted with the preferred berry producing scions of his favorite, the Illinois Everbearing Mulberry.

In addition to collecting berries, we supplemented our diet and the income at that time by trapping and hunting. Always looking to learn about a new "set", Dad was constantly alert to any new ideas about trapping. At some point he acquired a small book titled *Fox Trapping* written by A. R. Harding and published in 1906 (Harding 1906). As a publication, it was innocuous, being the collected, more or less ordered, ramblings of an old fox trapper. The work is grammatically weak and it was loosely organized but the thoughts - however awkwardly expressed - were effective.

Dad ordered this book to learn more about fox trapping and he did. It contained some interesting ideas about the psychology of the fox, his habits, and his innate curiosity. It stressed the need to understand the quarry before attempting to outsmart it by tempting it into a trap.

Weighing the value of the ideas that book contained against its unschooled presentation, Dad reached some surprising conclusions. That trapper's ramblings showed him that anyone can write down and publish their ideas. He realized that he need meet no educational requirements before writing. And most important of all – there is nothing to fear about either the act or the product of writing. That book, short and disorganized, taught Dad a lesson he would never forget: do not fear writing. If that old trapper could do it, then so could he.

Back to the mulberries. Each year Dad would meet with this character named Big Al for their annual mulberry eating contest. Bolstered by courage from reading *Fox Trapping*, and grammar be damned, he was inspired to record this experience and wrote *The Mulberry Eating Contest*, describing this singular ritual. Precisely when he wrote this piece is unknown. Most likely it was between 1950 and 1960, the period in which the slumbering botanist within him awakened sleepy-eyed only to discover a slumbering author as a bed partner.

Dad did not date this piece; it could as easily have come from his childhood as from his later adult life in Chesterfield. Other than the fact that Big Al drove a truck - not yet common when Dad was a boy - the only real clue may be his description of Big Al pulling into "my driveway". Perhaps this suggests a driveway from an unspecified time in his boyhood, but more likely he meant the driveway on the Chesterfield homestead. Nonetheless, this stands as one of his first personally authored pieces. It is an anecdote done in a dialog format. The explicit focus is on mulberries as being good to eat and the implicit message is on the use of natural foodstuffs as an important part of the diet.

At the same time, Dad began to experiment with nut trees. Pecans and walnuts, he learned, would also respond positively to grafting, but the grafts were more difficult to do and the percentage of successful takes was lower. But he figured that if he made a hundred grafts and only two survived, he was still successful. This minor "difficulty" with low percentage success rates did not deter him in the least. The way he figured it, if he wanted more successes, then he would just graft two hundred instead.

While complacently munching on his grafted mulberries, he set out on a lifelong quest for better nuts of all kinds. Mentally he contrasted the immediate gratification of mulberries to the delayed gratification of nuts, which naturally came packaged neatly into shells that allowed for essentially effortless storage possibilities. Recalling his childhood experience of eating bad apples all winter, and his appreciation of the storage capabilities of nuts, he also began to wonder about human relationships with these environmental gifts. As his thinking grew more and more broad, he decided, again, to record his thoughts and experiences in written format. He wrote *Man, the Seed Eater* in this early period of experimentation on his Chesterfield farm. This prose piece he wrote in an explanatory format. Again, I do not know the absolute date of creation, but it is clear that his temporal target spanned from his boyhood until the present with gratuitous generalizations about overall human adaptation.

The motivation for the next piece appears to be the annual tree planting that was part of the routine he inherited from his Grandmother. In this essay style piece he recalls working with her in the same endeavor. The article *Why Plant that Tree* he dated August, 1980, but its temporal placement is in 1929, when he was 10 years old. An interesting story on the surface, it reflects several more deeply rooted ideas. First, his strong relationship with his Grandma and his appreciation of family shines through. Second, his patience is apparent in his acceptance of things that will not mature for nearly a generation. Third, his willingness to invest energy now for the future and his unselfishness are equally apparent.

Fourth, on the wall over his desk was a small plaque that read "When you pray for potatoes, have a hoe in your hand", extolling self help as a virtue. His willingness to plant now for the future is the embodiment of that saying. Finally, *Why Plant that Tree* illustrates that he is confident in his ability to control the future if you work hard and are patient enough to wait for the results.

The final piece from this time period, *The Slick Robin*, is another anecdotal reminiscence of his days with Grandma. The authorship date of this piece is unclear but the temporal placement clearly is in the late 1920s when he was about 8 or 10 years old. In this piece, Grandma teaches him a lesson in patience and in humor. I cannot help but think exchanges like this were at least in part the origin of his adult wit.

Dad's writings of this period were free flowing and did not target any audience. He prepared these works for personal gratification and not for anyone else to read. The style is purely his, affected by few external forces, and it reflects his internal desire to record something for his own later use. He wrote these works without a recognition of, or an appreciation for, an external audience.

In *Coming to America*, Dad relates that when he was 10, he began to learn how to hunt and to trap to supplement the family income; when I was about 10, he reckoned that it was time to pass these skills on to me – time for me to begin to contribute to the family income. Trapping is a routine thing, locating runs, setting traps, running them sometimes twice a day, replacing them, preparing the pelts, selling them, and repeating the process. Over the years we did develop some unique sets which I will describe at another time.

Hunting was another aspect of gathering what you could from the land. Dad always kept at least two English Setters. These were magnificent dogs, well tempered, good with children, friendly, and absolutely superb at their hunting skill. Dad worked with them and honed them to perfection; they lived for the hunt. He was widely known for the prowess of his dogs. We called them by affectionate names like Freckles, Muggs, and Poncho[2]; they were part of our family.

Living in the country we had game to ourselves. We never overhunted or abused the resource; it was as much a part of our world as anything else. In fact, Dad often hatched and raised young pheasants, chukkers, quail and other game birds and released them in the off seasons to breed in the wild. It would have pleased Grandmother that we took from, and we gave back to, nature.

But the city hunters soon found us. They would appear in their 1950s station wagons full of brand new Browning shotguns, half trained dogs, and coolers of beer and they would hunt on our land with impunity. They did not ask permission and being a local community, we did not have the enforcement

---

2   Freckles was so named because she was pure white with small reddish brown dots all over; she was the mother of most of our later dogs, all of which she trained and all of which were superb hunters, just like Mom. Muggs, one of her sons, we named after the monkey on the popular Dave Garroway TV show: J. Fredd Muggs. Poncho – I never knew where that one came from. I always suspected Poncho Villa.

to prevent them. They decimated our game, turning a well balanced natural harmony into chaos.

One day, Dad heard of a hunting dog contest and he decided to enter our dogs. All the city hunters showed up with their fine equipment: expensive hunting coats, camouflage hats, LL Bean boots, station wagons, mirror sunglasses, specially loaded shotgun shells, and inflated egos. While they oiled their guns and polished their stocks, and told their standard lies, their dogs stood in perfect three leg stances, with right front foot 4 inches above the ground, noses pointing forward, tails to the rear, and quivering – just like they had been trained - with well rehearsed anticipation.

Dad and I arrived in his Chevy Bel Air with the two dogs in the trunk, Muggs and Poncho if I remember correctly. He opened the trunk and the dogs leapt out like bullets fired from those pretty shotguns, made a few cursory licks of thanks for the opportunity to hunt again, pissed on a few tires, and immediately raced past the statue dogs as though they were not there. They streaked down the hedge row, suddenly braking their churning legs, sliding to a halt, and when the dust settled, were locked on point at a distance of about 150 meters. They had the birds. I knew that. So did Dad. All the statue dogs suspected something was up. The only ones not aware of what was happening were the LL Bean hunters, still adjusting their equipment and thumbing their gun sights like a gaggle of Audie Murphys in an old movie. Dad whistled and the dogs, on perfect cue and in perfect unison, sprang into the birds as one, raising the entire covey into flight. Dad did not fire; following his lead, I did not either. The dogs turned around and looked at us wondering what was wrong. The statue dogs continued to tremble nervously. They looked scared, and I quietly wondered to myself whether they had ever heard the unmistakable sound of a covey of startled quail taking flight before.

Dad turned back to the car, opened the rear, and in wink, the dogs were back in the trunk, albeit confused. We got in the car and went home. That was the last hunting dog contest we ever attended. For all I know, the statue dogs may still be there, wondering what happened that day when those birds had made such a terrible noise.

The Mulberry Eating Contest

An old battered pick-up truck coughed and wheezed along the road, slowed down, and lurched into my driveway. The windshield was cracked and the tail pipe dragged. I knew it was Big Al.

Big Al was here to challenge me to a mulberry eating contest. I had beaten him last year. You didn't beat Big Al easy or often in any kind of an eating contest. I wished I hadn't eaten so much dinner.

Al's hired man once told me that Al ate a dozen ears of sweet corn every day for dinner. If you asked Al why he ate a dozen ears of corn and only gave his mules six ears each, he would explain that the mules shared the work pulling the plow but he had to do all the steering.

Al stopped the truck, turned off the motor, turned, placed his feet on the ground and said:

"They ripe?"

"Yeah."

"You ready?"

"Yeah."

"Then spread it out."

We unrolled a sheet of white plastic under the mulberry tree, shook the tree, gathered the four corners of the plastic together, and tipped the ripe mulberries to the center. It sure looked like a big pile to me. I wished again I hadn't eaten so much dinner.

We sat down cross-legged facing each other. Using the bill of his cap, Al cut the pile down the middle. He took out his false teeth and dropped them into his shirt pocket; then he took off his spectacles and dropped them into his other shirt pocket.

"What for, Al?"

"Can't taste as good with 'em in, can't swaller near as big a gob either. My ears go up and down when I swaller and the spectacles chafe my ears."

"You know the rules?"
"Yeah."

Al knew we only had one rule: Just sit down and eat more mulberries than the other guy.

"You sure got a good, straight cut, Al."

"Yeah. You ready?"

"Wait a couple of minutes."

"What's holding you up?"

"Wait a couple of minutes and let the pissants run out of the pile."

"We didn't do that last year."

"Yeah, I know we didn't, and you ate about a pint of pissants last year."

"Did I, well I'll be doggoned, I remember I sure filled up quick."

"They're gone now, Al."

"Fine, let's go."

"I'm ready."

Fourteen minutes later, Al's pile was gone. He belched. Wiped the back of his hand across his mouth, then looked up at me. I still had about a pint and a half of berries left.

"You give?"

"Yeah, I'm loaded."

"We gotta shake the other tree."

"Why?"

"I need a couple of quarts to eat after supper."

"Yeah, sure Al, we'll shake it. Soon as I rest a minute."

Man: the Seed Eater

by
MYRON S. NIXON

Sometime, somewhere back in man's long evolutionary past, he became a seed eater.

Plants store food in the form of protein in and around the embryo, or seed. Hence the newly formed seed was now able to sprout, grow roots, stems, and leaves. Now it could exist totally independent of the mother plant. It is thought that man discovered many seeds had a good taste and furnished much needed nutrition. Man had, at this point, taken a giant step to avoid winter starvation.

Some seeds could be stored and kept until the long winter ended.

Man learned to eat many parts of plants. He ate leaves, stems, roots, tubers, seeds, and seed coatings. But most of these plant parts had to be eaten immediately. A few could be stored for a limited length of time.

When nut trees were discovered early man successfully overcame another major obstacle. Nuts could be stored easily and came to him enclosed nicely within an air tight shell. All he needed to do was gather them and hide them from rodents. He soon learned to pile nuts upon a large flat stone, crib around them with other stones and top the entire mass off with more stones.

Archaeologists are now finding that the American Indian was rather adept at nut storage. They simply dug pits in the ground and buried the nuts there. It is thought that the pits were dug in the ground inside their tepees.

My personal love for nuts began when my memory began, in the early 1920s. Hazel nuts, hickory and black walnut were gathered in large quantities each fall. All were good but black walnuts were my favorite. My mother made cookies, cakes, and even baked bread using black walnut kernels. And if one hasn't eaten sweet potatoes baked with black walnut kernels sprinkled over them he has missed half his life.

Back in the mid sixties, I planted and grafted about 150 black walnut trees. I often think about how I used to go to the barn on a rainy day and eat black walnuts all afternoon. Now if we could have had the easy cracking varieties we have now . . . one could become sick so much quicker.

Why Plant That Tree, Grandma? (August 1970)

By

Myron S. Nixon

With spring tree-planting time just around the corner, most of us have our plans made; and we can hardly wait to start. I suppose you all have heard the standard alibis for not planting, such as, "Takes too long to bear," and "I'll have to mow around them, if I plant in my yard". One lady bemoaned the fact that she was 37; and if the tree took five years to bear, she would be 42 before it bore. I wondered how old she would be in five years if she didn't plant the tree.

I once asked my beloved Grandmother this same question, "Why plant this tree?" The answer I got is still stamped in my memory as if it were yesterday.

We were inseparable, Grandma and I. We gathered nuts, berries, roots, greens, and wild fruit along with our domestic crop. Grandma always had a few peach or apricot seeds, or some horseradish roots in her apron to plant as we made our journeys through the woods and meadows. She had sharp eyes and often spied a muskrat or raccoon track that I missed as we went along.

One day we were planting some seedling cherries. (We always planted trees in late August and picked all the leaves off. I don't know why she picked this time or method; I always supposed that was planting time in Northern Europe, from whence she came.)

We planted the tree, and I went to the straw stack and returned with a sack of straw for mulch. Three times I went to the spring, returning with a gourd full of pure, sweet water; each time Grandma drank deeply and poured the remainder around our tree. As we paused to rest, I asked, Grandma, at your age of 78, why do you plant this tree?" She brushed her wispy hair back with her hand and gazed out across the prairie; then she smiled at me. I knew Grandma had a story to tell, and when Grandma told a story--everyone listened. She told of hunger and poverty in Europe, of starvation and oppression. She told of crossing the great ocean at nine years old, of a baby sister who died at sea, and of a terrible storm that damaged the rigging of the ship which forced them to stay "a long time at a Terrible Cold Place." (I never knew, but I have always wondered where.). [FYI: He eventually settled on Greenland as their probable "terrible cold" stopping over point].

Then her old face lit up and she smiled as she told of landing here and coming to Central Illinois. She told of the great forests of nuts and berries to be had for the picking, and of such a bountiful harvest beyond all her wildest dreams. Someone had planted all this just for her, she had said, and she had lived in great abundance for nearly seventy years. (I remember the thought struck me that maybe all these Indians weren't bad guys at all, for they must have planted these trees for Grandma.) "Now," she said, "we must plant more so you and all your children will have plenty in times to come." At ten, it was hard for me to envision ever being seventy, but it gave me a warm feeling inside to think we were planting trees for me; and I remember as I washed for supper that evening my mother asked me if had been helping Grandma. I replied, "No Mama; Grandma has been helping me."

Chesterfield, Illinois, August 1970

The Slick Robin

by
Myron Nixon

At Grandma's house the yard fence ran along about forty feet from the north kitchen window. One old white oak post had a hole in the top, with cavity about ten inches deep. A blue bird nested there every spring, and Grandma thought the world of that blue bird.

As soon as the bluebird returned in the spring Grandma peeked into that hole every morning to see if any eggs had been laid.

One morning when Grandma went out to gather eggs and feed the chickens I put a robin egg into the hole, wrapped it in my handkerchief and very gently placed it into the nest. I watched closely and when she looked in that morning she paused, scratched her head, then looked in again. I could almost read her thoughts — now why would that robin lay an egg in a bluebird's nest, and how did that robin ever get into that little hole?

I was over-joyed to think that I had fooled her, for Grandma was not easily fooled, and tricky as a mule colt. She made no mention of the bluebird's nest at dinner, and of course I was anxiously awaiting any comment. I tried to get a comment out of her telling a story about a robin that had somehow fallen into a bucket of axle grease that morning when I was greasing the wagon wheels, saying, "That robin was so slick he could have crawled though a mouse hole." She was absolutely non-committal, no response whatever.

That evening I went to the creek to set some bank lines, intending to stay all night and perhaps catch some channel catfish. A thunder storm drove me home about midnight.

I jumped into bed and immediately jumped back out. Some creature was in my bed and I was sure that it had bitten me! I hurriedly lit the lamp, and with the lamp in one hand and the stove poker in the other, I gingerly searched the bed. The creature I found was a ball of cockle-burrs about the size of a goose egg, along with a scrap of paper bearing four words — "Robin been here too."

VI. DISCOVERING AN AUDIENCE: INTA, NAFEX, & THE POMONA (1960-1973)

In the decade+ from 1950 to 1963, Dad's skills nurturing trees and shrubs increased steadily. Now with land to cultivate, his interests gravitated toward the fruits and nuts that were important to him in his boyhood: walnuts, pecans, hickories, mulberries, and for fun, some ornamentals. He noticed diseases and irregularities in some of the plants and set out to find solutions. He noticed, for example, that wild hickories were not susceptible to root diseases that other trees, like pecans, were. He struck on the idea of combining the best of both: he grafted pecan tops onto the root systems of wild hickories. The result was a disease resistant tree that bore 'hicans', a cross between the hardiness of a hickory and the taste of a pecan with a slight hickory flavor. But, unlike the densely shelled hickory, the nut had a thin shell, more like a pecan.

With time he honed these skills. He also met and talked with others who had similar interests, sharing with them the things he had discovered in his experimentations and learning from their successes and failures as well. Networking came easily for an affable, witty man who also had a curiosity about nature.

Eventually he came into contact with members of the INTA (Illinois Nut Tree Association). This expanded his universe of contacts beyond neighbors and friends to an academic and organizational level. He began to meet with Professors, Teachers, nursery specialists and others who belonged to this group and he discovered sources of information that had not previously been available to him. I do not recall him mentioning any journal or other publication of INTA although surely they must have had some published medium.

As organizational and individual communications became more frequent among those interested in botanical issues, a need developed to meet periodically to talk about experiments, results (good and bad), techniques of grafting, *etc*. One result of this sharing of information was the formation of NAFEX, the North American Fruit EXplorers. As a charter member, Dad, in league with several of his botanically like minded friends, developed a journal, the *Pomona*, as a means to communicate ideas, experiences, and stories among themselves. Using the mail, they could transcend the physical distances that separated them from one another. They used the *Pomona* to maintain contact in the periods between their irregular meetings.

Dad's initial 'professional' writings were for publication in this journal and consisted of prose pieces, sometimes done as dialog, relating events he had experienced with fruits, nuts and berries. Although his writings of the 1950-1960 period were independent and opportunistic with little external influence, his works from 1960-1973 show increasing skill as a result of interaction with other amateurs and professionals in an ever widening peer group. The earlier writings targeted no audience; the later writings did. He now understood that his words on the page must speak as eloquently, or more so, as those he uttered in public. After all, he could always deny he said something but if it were in writing . . . The contributors to the *Pomona* were his example, his peers; the readers of the *Pomona* were his audience consisting both of amateurs like himself and the occasional interested professional member. They were writing for each other and this was new ground for him as an author – and maybe all of them - a literary landscape complete with an audience.

One of the stylistic details yet to be developed was dating all his written materials. Of the following five pieces, none are dated. I grouped them here because of their similarity in style and content; they all represent his early writings produced in the 1960-1973 timeframe. A before B . . .

The first is titled *Good Fruit, No Sweat, No Spray*. In prose style, it presents what amounts to a testimonial to the Illinois Everbearing Mulberry, his old favorite. He wrote it in the present tense. Three elements are noteworthy. First, his recognition of the audience is explicit as he extols readers to contact him directly for scion wood. Second, he includes a quote from an academic from the University of Illinois, obviously attempting to elevate the quality of his text and of his circle of acquaintances. Third, at the end of the piece, his inherent down home humor surfaces as his personal trademark.

The next piece also from the same period he titled *Better Mulberries for Wildlife*. The overall focus of this prose style work is to encourage mulberry grafting for the ultimate purpose of attracting more wildlife. Again there is a pitch to the reader to contact him for scion wood and again his humor will not be denied.

Mulberry Propagation provides instructions on how to graft mulberries. Again not dated, he wrote it in the present tense. Done in an instructive prose style, this is a very informative work providing the *Pomona* reader with the necessary information to successfully cut scion wood and propagate mulberries themselves.

The final two pieces from this period change direction. He switches from his early favorite, the mulberry, to the black walnut. Done in a prose style, *Black Walnuts* provides the *Pomona* reader with information about the origin of modern black walnuts, the development of better varieties over time, and information on the particular varieties that were available.

The final piece switches in temporal referent back twenty years to his early days when he learned grafting to the present (at the time of writing). In *Improving Black Walnuts* he notes the membership of INTA and references their interaction among each other. Showing an interest in, and an understanding of, plant genetics, he advocates natural cloning within a small plant community, and evaluating the offspring, as an alternate method to isolate yet another better, higher yielding, or more tasty variety of Black Walnut.

Good Fruit, No Sweat, No Spray

By Myron S. Nixon

If someone button-holed you and tried to sell you a tree that had all of the following points, you would probably call the better business bureau and report him as a fraud. You might even call the boys wearing the white suits and carrying butterfly nets.

Imagine a tree that bears thirty to forty gallons of delicious berries each year, over a period of about six weeks. Berries that are excellent for pies, jellies, or for eating fresh from the tree. This tree ripens it's fruit at an opportune time, shortly after strawberry season ends, thus filling a large gap in spring fruit harvesting. This tree needs no spray, has no insect or disease problems; this tree needs no pruning or care whatever! This same tree attracts and feeds all wildlife for at least six weeks of the year. Birds and animals love its fruit. This same tree bears fruit sweet enough that it can be consumed fresh, or made into pies, and eaten by diabetics without further sweetening.

The name of this tree is, *Illinois Everbearing Mulberry*, and you can have as many of these trees as you wish. For free! I'm not kidding you. All you have to do is write to me for scions. Sure, I expect you to reimburse me for postage and handling, but the wood is free.

A recent letter from everybody's friend at the Univ. of Illinois, Urbana, Mr. J. C. McDaniel, informs me, and I quote Dr. McDaniel:

> "All things considered, Ill. Everbearing is still probably the best edible fruited mulberry for Ill."

He also lists the only fault he can find with it. Again I quote:

> "The principal fault I find is that the birds love it so well that you need at least two trees to get enough for yourself any one day, and the birds get up early enough to beat you to the ripe fruits".

I might add here that mulberries have, over the years, been much maligned because of the bad habit birds have of eating the berries and then flying over the clothes line, spattering the clothes with their droppings. While this is partially true, I think we should remember that mulberries have taken much more of the blame than is due them. We tend to blame the mulberry tree, when in truth it is often the fault of, blackberries, dewberries, grapes, wild cherries, and polk berries. Probably more that I can't think of. With the advent of gas and electric clothes dryers, I think we can now safely lay this old cliche to rest.

Better Mulberries for Wildlife

By Myron S. Nixon

The Illinois Everbearing Mulberry is, in my opinion, the best mulberry I have ever seen. The fruit is large, sweet, and has a zesty flavor. Not at all like most wild mulberries. Wild mulberries always seem to have a watery, insipid taste, or taste as if they had been dipped in cheap perfume.

The excellent flavor, along with the extended ripening season, and the massive amount of fruit produced is, I believe, the main reason it appeals so strongly to wildlife. About twenty years ago I topworked several large wild trees in my pasture to Illinois Everbearing. Now I'm sure glad that I did.

I have observed these trees closely over the years, and have noticed they are frequently visited by deer, rabbit, opossum, groundhog, and raccoon. Once I had the good fortune to be in the right place at the right time to observe an old coyote as she brought her three pups to one of these grafted trees. They ate the ripe berries from the ground for about ten minutes. On another occasion when I walked under one of these trees, and began to casually eat the ripe fruit a grey fox jumped out of the tree, nearly on top of me. Came very nearly causing me to suffer a cardiac arrest. I think I did have a light stroke. My laundry isn't back yet.

In some of the larger trees I have topworked only a few limbs to Illinois Everbearing. Birds and animals never fail to eat the fruit from the top worked portion of the tree first. One seldom finds many berries on the ground under the topworked trees either.

Birds of all kinds flock to these topworked trees, almost totally neglecting the wild trees. Observing this, my little grand daughter once observed, "No kids or birds don't like mulberries". A bit of wisdom from a three year old.

It is my opinion that if we can persuade more of our neighbors to topwork wild mulberry trees to better varieties, we may, in the not too distant future, recover some of our depleted wildlife. As a lifetime hunter and trapper, I feel that it is my duty, as well as a privilege, to spend a few hours each spring in an effort to improve the general environment.

Joseph M. Nixon

Each spring I always cut an abundance of scion wood from my Illinois Everbearing mulberry trees, and I would be glad to share it with anyone who would like to graft it on his own particular tree. There will be no charge for this wood. Just to show you I'm trying to treat you right, I'll even give you a couple of weeks to shop around and see if you can find it cheaper somewhere else.

Mulberry Propagation

By Myron S. Nixon

The mulberry is, in my opinion, one of the easiest of all plants to propagate. It ranks among the althea bushes and apple trees in ease of propagation. Success comes readily if one follows a few simple rules of procedure.

Spring grafting with dormant scions is the method most often used. I always save scions from my Illinois Everbearing trees. I cut them in February or early March and store them inside a plastic bag along with a wet napkin to keep them moist. I put the bag into the refrigerator. Thus the scions are kept alive by the moisture from the damp napkin and the cool environment of the refrigerator prevents the buds from swelling.

I might add here that I have often grafted mulberries successfully by simply cutting scions from one tree and immediately inserting them into another. No dormancy; no refrigeration; no storage. The percentage of "takes" is not as high as when dormant scions are used. However, in an emergency such as when you run out of scions, this method can be of great value.

Mulberries can be grafted any time beginning April 1st, until about the 4th of July. You should never try to set scions, when the stock exudes sticky, milky sap. Wait until it quits. This milky substance will get into the graft unions and ferment, causing the graft to fail. As soon as the stock leafs out, it will quit.

The bark graft or the whip and tongue graft seem to be the best for mulberries. If you don't know how to make these two grafts, simply attend a grafting demonstration at any spring Illinois Nut Tree Association meeting, or come here and I will guarantee that I can teach you both grafts in about five minutes.

Rootstock used for grafting can be any seedling mulberry. They grow almost anywhere: along fence rows, in back alleys, in pastures and fields, and even in state parks. I usually spend one afternoon each spring grafting mulberries in my pasture and in pastures belonging to my neighbors. I carry a pocket full of scions and an aluminum step ladder and set scions above where the cattle can reach. My neighbors are very tolerant of me and go out of their way to humor me. Sometimes I wonder about this.

Some follow-up care is necessary. I usually go back at least twice during the summer and cut all scion growth back to about 12-14 inches. If allowed to grow too long, the wind will break them out. Until the second year, the unions are not very strong.

So what's holding you up? If you want more birds, more animals, more big sweet mulberries, then get with it. Its the time to cut scion wood, now.

Black Walnuts

By Myron S. Nixon

Dr. William Butler, a celebrated physician of the sixteenth century, once said of the strawberry:

Doubtless God could have made a better strawberry, but doubtless he never did.

I hope the good doctor would not mind too much if I should apply this same logic to the black walnut. The texture of the walnut kernel, along with it's divine flavor, has long been a great favorite with those who love nuts of all kinds.

Black walnut kernels retain their delicate flavor under practically all conditions. They may be baked in cakes or cookies, added as toppings to ice cream, stirred into Jell-O, or best of all, they may be cracked and eaten out at the barn on rainy days. Grandmother sprinkled black walnuts over sweet potatoes as they simmered in the oven. Try it, you won't be sorry you did. It should be remembered, however, that picking out the kernels from those old seedling walnuts was a long and tedious job. Those old nuts had thick shells and heavy partitions inside their shells. All of that, however, has been changed.

We now have thin shelled varieties that are easily cracked, and the kernels may be recovered in much larger chunks. We also have the single lobed varieties that when cracked the kernels may be recovered whole and intact. This change for the better did not come about easily or quickly. A man named J. W. Thomas of King of Prussia, Pennsylvania, reputedly was the first man to graft black walnuts successfully. He selected a local seedling that was of good size, well flavored, rather thin shelled and cracked easily. This was in the late eighteen hundreds. He named the resulting clone Thomas. The Thomas black walnut is still with us today.

J. W. Thomas showed the way. He proved to the world that it could be done, and his technology has been passed on to us. Improvements on his technology have come to us over the past hundred years in the form of better grafting materials. However, grafting black walnuts is still not easy.

Joseph M. Nixon

Black walnuts have been gathered over most of North America and each gatherer seems to develop a liking for a favorite tree. Dozens of these favorite tress have now been propagated but the search still goes on, and will do so for perhaps another hundred years.

At a recent gathering of Illinois nut tree enthusiasts, I asked several members my favorite question:

> If you had room at your home for only one black walnut tree, which one would you plant?

I was astonished at the answers I received. Each person gave me a different answer. This seems to indicate that there is no one particular clone that stands head and shoulders above all the others. For instance, ELMER MEYER bears the thinnest shelled nut known and has the highest percent ratio of kernel to shell. It also has an unwanted trait. It is the latest to come into pistillate bloom in the spring. Consequently an early fall frost brings about a total crop loss. Another instance, the THROP when cracked yields it's kernels whole and intact. The THROP tree, however, never seems to bear a heavy crop. In another instance, the MULEMAN bears every year, yields good crops, the nuts crack out whole with the kernels intact, but the nut is small, about the size of a medium sized filbert.

So perhaps we should revise out thinking, modify our standards, and learn to appreciate what we have, not what we wish we had.

Improving Black Walnuts

By Myron Nixon

Some twenty years ago I learned the art of grafting trees. Mr. R. B. Best of Eldred, Illinois, befriended me and he and his assistant, Cleo Holterfield, both took me in hand teaching me the whip and tongue, and the bark, or veneer, graft. Mr. Best, along with J. C. McDaniel of the University of Illinois, Urbana, were indeed two giants in the field of Horticulture that I was very fortunate to know at that time. Both were great humanitarians, also. Mr. Best took a great personal interest in growing and improving pecans. My own interest later turned to black walnuts.

Members of I. N. T. A. [Illinois Nut Tree Association] have long been urged to search for better varieties of black walnuts, pecans, hickories, hicans, and other wild varieties of nuts. This search has been of great benefit to all of us, as many better varieties have come to light, scions have been exchanged and distributed throughout our membership.

Now with the advances in technology that have come about in recent years it would seem that we could do even more to further our advances in the search for better clones. The science of genetics has advanced far enough for all of us to see and understand that the improvement of varieties of black walnuts might well be carried out by breeding the best clones together. In short, breeding the best to the best. No, I don't advocate that we all take the field with our spyglasses, plastic bags, *etc.* Few of us have the time or the technology to cross-pollinate by hand. What I do mean is that most of us in I. N. T. A. do have from six to a dozen trees, of different varieties, growing close enough together to cross pollinate naturally. All we need to do is plant a few nuts from these grafted trees each spring.

When these seedlings come into bearing, we can then evaluate them as to quality, hoping to find a better clone than the parent. If we don't find them to be better than the parent tree, it is a simple process to top work them to a better variety. Actually no time is lost in the process. It would seem that we would be much more apt to find a better clone in this manner than searching in the wild.

No, I don't advocate discontinuing our search in the wild for better nut producing varieties. I do, however, think that we should add this seedling idea to our methods already in progress.

VII. SCHOOL DAYS – AGAIN (ca. 1973 - 1980)

"I must conclude an Anthropologist does not have an easy life, is underpaid, misunderstood, and often scorned, even by his own colleagues, but I would give my right arm to be one" (Myron S. Nixon, October 9, 1973).

We know that Dad went to Chesterfield High School. Once while exploring some long stored away boxes, we found a faded previously maroon and white colored High School letter "C" which, Dad eventually admitted, was his. He told us that he earned it playing on the Chesterfield High School tennis team.

The High School in Chesterfield occupied a spot in the south part of town. Attached to it, to the south and extending to the east, was an oval shaped, dirt surfaced, quarter mile running track with grounds for field sports – presumably shot put, javelin, high hump, and related activities - inside and just beyond it. The entire high school, grounds, track, and all sold into private holding and the buyers ultimately demolished it as I grew up.

We know that Dad went to Chesterfield High, but we learned little else about his early education. Over the years we learned only a few things about Mom's education. She once related to my sister that she was active in GAA (Girls' Athletic Association) while in High School, which we assume was in Alton, Illinois. Later, she and my Sister were involved in bowling, bicycle riding, croquet, badminton and other family type sports. She also played softball and was an accomplished enough pitcher that her grandson, at age 5, declared that she was good enough to play on the Old Ladies Minor League. My sister remembers her as "very athletic". She was a self learner, a hands on person, who taught herself to type, to refinish and reupholster furniture, to plan and make various crafts, and the all important game of Poker that served her very well at family get togethers (like the one where she met Dad?). She marked the passage of time by watching her children grow and by the increasingly severe rheumatoid arthritis that in the beginning precluded her from any strenuous sports and, in the end, nearly all physical activities.

When the time came for my sister and I to go to school, we attended the Chesterfield Grade School at the east end of the track once part of the High School compound. We walked about three quarters of a mile to school – yes, actually sometimes in the snow. Our house, the last on the western limits of

Chesterfield, was the furthest address from which children had to walk to school. Dave, our neighbor to the west, in "unincorporated" Chesterfield, waved to us from his seat on the bus everyday. On occasion a neighbor passing in a vehicle would pick us up and gave us a relief ride rescuing us from the walk home, but such luck was not dependable.

After the sixth grade, I rode a bus to neighboring (and larger) Carlinville, to their Junior High and High Schools (Carlinville Consolidated High School District- CCHS). It was twelve miles distant. Abandoned, the Chesterfield High School closed many years before. In two years, my sister followed me to CCHS, also riding the bus, probably the same one, probably still driven by Carl.

In those early days, we had one phone in the house, a wooden, box shaped device that had a crank on the right side. My sister remembers that our ring was "two longs and a short". When you wanted to call someone, you picked up the earpiece that hung on a hook on the left side, cranked the generator on the right side a turn or two, and in response to your signal, the switchboard operator would answer. You then told her who it was that you wanted to call and she would put the appropriate plugs (she would "operate" it) into the switchboard. As often as not, she would 'pike' on the line, absent mindedly neglecting to remove her wire after she made your connection. The neighbors heard all the signals too, and could – and did – listen in on your conversations which my Sister compares to a rudimentary form of "hacking" *sans* computers. It was a small town. National security issues were rare.

Dad built a little corner shelf just inside the front door by the phone. Not long after that, he bought a radio and put it on that shelf. This was as close to an entertainment center as the technology of the day would allow.

In the evening we would listen to that radio, as a family enjoying the Amos and Andy Show, The Lone Ranger, The Shadow and other radio entertainment classics. Some time after that, Dad came home with a television, a black and white, rabbit eared contraption that sometimes worked and sometimes didn't. When it did work, we would make popcorn in the evenings after dinner and the whole family would watch Ed Sullivan, Red Skelton, Lawrence Welk, Milton Berle, I've Got a Secret, What's My Line, and other popular shows of the day. On Saturday nights my sister and I stayed up until the Indian and the test pattern came on, accompanied by the incessant nonstop ringing that would eventually drive us to bed. Mom and Dad at that time, and now my sister some decades later, still relate the story of one of the local networks broadcasting a "Technical Difficulties" placard with instructions to "Please Stand By", which, they relate laughingly, I obediently did. Hey, at least I could read and follow instructions.

The cumulative effect of first a phone, then a radio, then television, and then ongoing education put my sister and me into a long learning curve leading inexorably to the computer age. We were curious about nearly everything. We had learned how to learn and we wanted more. Mom and Dad, of course, fostered these feelings in us and quietly began a campaign to get both of us to go to college after high school. We did not recognize it at the time, but their campaign was continuous, unrelenting, and sometimes overpowering but, with clarity in retrospect, I'm glad we fell for it.

But there was an unexpected fallout. My sister and I began to expect Mom and Dad to become more interested in education too. After all, they had taught us that school and learning were the natural order of things. So together, we began a school pressure program on them equally as seditious as the one they had quietly foist onto us. After all, of his own volition Dad had made a deal that if we went to school now, he would too, but . . . later. Designed as a ploy to motivate us, we turned it on him and on Mom. In response, Mom redoubled her interest in church and the community.

At this same time, Dad was becoming more and more adept at grafting trees and experimenting with his ever expanding botanical menagerie. He began to meet and talk to others with the same interests and slowly became part of a network of plant hobbyists and professionals. To communicate with them across both space and time required that he put some of his ideas on paper. The not very unconscious prodding of two children steeped in education combined with his growing base of educated colleagues, spurred him to begin to experiment more earnestly with writing some of his ideas.

Soon his network grew as above, culminating in NAFEX and the *Pomona*, their journal. Dad's earliest writings were remembrances and musings about his various experiences with fruit and nut trees; many appeared as occasional essays in the *Pomona*. As above, Dad did not date many of these early works and I group them here because they represent the same approximate time. Many were also anecdotal, not explanatory or scientific. Often they were unintentionally anthropological in nature, equally often with a tangential moral message, indiscreetly packaged in humor. Without benefit of advanced schooling, many of these are strikingly reminiscent of his upbringing and personality and I believe are a near direct reflection of things taught to him by his Mother and Grandmother. Some have charm, some wit, some a meaning that only he could fathom from his own childhood, and some tell implied stories about his Mother and Grandmother that help us all understand them even though we never knew them.

As my sister and I finished college, we began to insist and then demand that Dad live up to his promise and do the same. We figured the "later" that he promised had now arrived. At first, he laughed it off, shrugged and changed the subject, instructing us to go back to school. I cannot remember how many times we heard: "I'm too old to go to school" which prompted us to routinely explain yet again all about adult education and night classes. He even tried "I can't afford the tuition" to which we responded that he was entitled to full support under the GI Bill. We, however, willingly went back to school until there was no more school to attend. In the face of incessant nagging, Dad finally gave in; he decided to attempt a college course. After all, Lewis and Clark College (L&C) was just down the road; he was retired now and had time on his hands, and; he was curious about learning more about plant anatomy, propagation, genetics, and nurturing. He decided to give it a chance.

He did not yet know about the application and registration headaches to come and not wanting to give him any reason to falter, my sister and I kept quiet about those small but worrisome aspects of college life. Nonetheless, in 1973 he achieved acceptance and he managed to register at L&C in Godfrey, Illinois. Nervous about being a return student, he was full of doubt and trepidation. Just as he had said good bye to us on that first day of our first grade, we stood at the end of the driveway and waved goodbye to him as he drove away to his first night class. *Quid pro quo, Pater*. Had the "high five" been around at that time, my sister and I would have discretely waited until his taillights disappeared around the corner, then simultaneously jumped into the air and high fived.

Several things occurred that influenced his selection of a curriculum. To begin somewhat afield, when I graduated in 1969, I had specialized in Microbiology and Biochemistry. That encouraged Dad to consider that his son was to become a serious scientist – not such a shoddy accomplishment he must have thought to himself. Maybe even just like Jonas Salk. A good thing. But these silver clouds had a dark lining. Before my graduation I was plagued with "greetings" notices from the local draft board in Carlinville. Either Dad, or the University, or both, parried them one by one, arguing that I was on track to complete a degree program that could be useful in many contexts, including military, if they would only wait. This buying time lasted only until the day of my graduation when yet another notice appeared. I was drafted.

To Dad, this unwelcome interruption of my otherwise smooth degree track was absurd - recall his own misgivings about military service. But, he reasoned, I had reached a landmark in my studies so brief military service might not be such a bad thing. The years had diluted the bad memories of his own Army life. Anecdotal recollections of misadventures and old Army buddies filled the resulting void with more positive memories. My periodic reports of the oxymoronic intelligence of Basic Training, then AIT, and then further training at Fort Benning awakened these Rumplestiltskin nightmares in his mind. Amid these renewed and not so happy reveries came the notification that the Army was shipping me overseas for a tour of duty in Korea. I have no doubt that this caused a flood of memories of the Fijii Islands in his mind and rekindled memories of the waste of manpower and intellect that the Army previously had shown to him – like training him to be a jungle commando. I often wondered whether the feelings that engulfed him on that day I left for the service were similar to those felt by his Mother on the day he left for his own tour of duty.

When off duty at the medic station in Korea, I had a lot of free time and not much to do. Although never considering it before, I became interested in photography, purchased some very good equipment cheaply through the PX, and took many pictures of the people and the countryside, sending a stream of images homeward (prints & slides, digital cameras had yet to be invented). In the local markets, I bought souvenirs of the Asian culture and sent them home as well. Dad fixated. How do the people live? What do they eat? How do they grow all that rice? What do they do when there's a funeral? Are men or women the family leaders? What kind of livestock do they keep? How do they figure kinship? Have you ever ridden a water buffalo? Do they go to movies? Question after question, each one a cradle that birthed two more. I wondered if he were as insistent with the people of Fijii when he was there. And if so, why had they not eaten him?

When I returned in 1972, the SIU (Southern Illinois University) Department of Microbiology was not interested in my stale (three year old) understanding of the discipline, was not convinced that I could catch up by studying on my own, and would not readmit me into the very program of studies wherein I had excelled just a few years before. Representing some of the best minds from many countries, they were truly sorry about the American draft requirement but remained adamant that there was no place for me in the Life Sciences Building any more.

So, having been unwillingly thrust into the literal backwaters of Korean society, and having actually enjoyed living in it and being part of it for a year, I walked out of the Life Sciences building, took a right turn, and walked over to the Anthropology Department. They were happy to see me.

Perhaps it was my involvement in Anthropology, or a year in Korea, or his personal experiences in the jungles with the Fijii Islanders, or perhaps it was a combination of all these events that steered Dad through the early days of college. Almost all agree that deciding on a major is one of the toughest decisions that a new college student can face. But Dad did not face this problem; he did not have to choose a major - Anthropology picked him.

As a college student, Dad had to take many different classes, some of which must have seemed unnecessary to him. Ah, the General Studies curriculum. Nonetheless, included here are some of the papers, exams, essays and other documents he prepared while in school. As you read these pieces, keep in mind that until college, all of his writing was at his own volition and motivation. Once in school, the albatross of actual assignments and structured writing projects that came adorned with deadlines became apparent. And with all that came the previously unknown and very audacious phenomenon known as criticism from Instructors who actually graded his works. As the volume of his work increased, he became more and more adept at using words, sentences, paragraphs, and outlines to structure his ideas for effective presentation to this new and apparently unfriendly audience called Instructors.

One of his earliest works, *The Speech*, he prepared in about 1972 at the beginning of his first college classes. It appears that he wrote it for some sort of class in Contemporary Writing. It is an essay punctuated with dialog that he wrote in the present tense. It contains his familiar affability expressed in his own words as turning "a stranger into a friend".

Dad reveals an interesting detail in this work. My sister and I both believe that in at least some measure it was our incessant nagging that motivated him to return to school. Urgings that we both remember were rooted in a combination attitude of "You can do it" tempered with one of "Now its your turn". To the lady with the checkbook in the long black car, Dad offers an alternative explanation.

His attitude and approach to school begins another piece from that period which he titled *A Friend of My Friend*. This short prose work was prepared at about the same time and does not appear to have been an assignment. It ends with a typically humanistic turn. It also displays one of Dad's signature literary styles. It recounts an event that may or may not have actually happened. But whether it happened or not, he had a point to make. And in his mind, it was the point that counted, not the facts that, oh yeah, backed it up.

In addition to these pieces, several other written items represent this time of his life. Included are five essay exams, four book reviews, a written report of a marketing assignment interview, a correspondence from the SIU School of Humanities, and an essay on education that appears to be a self assigned "senior paper" in which he expresses his views on his own education in particular and on adult education in general.

His response to the examination paper dated October 9, 1973, demonstrates his continuing addiction to Anthropology. It appears to present an answer to some sort of human geography question. Another piece (ANTH 231, Nov 5, 1973) seems to have been his response to an Anthropology exam, but it is unclear whether this is the same class or not. The range of questions that elicited these responses would be typical of an Introduction to Anthropology course. The "Physical Anthropology" questions specifically focused on evolution and genetics. Given his proclivity for studies of genetics in plants, this must have provided him with considerable food for thought. Just like mulberries.

A November 6, 1974, paper focuses on the question of man and his environmental interactions culminating with examples from his own experiences. His interest in anthropological issues continues. In a November 26, 1974, essay he addresses the general question of fossil evidence for human evolution. I would imagine that he really enjoyed this segment of the class.

Delving into human interactions, his answer to a May 6, 1974, question explores rites of passage and marriage. He concludes that ". . . transition rights are all a bunch of baloney". Receiving a B/B- grade from the Instructor, this may not have been the perfect conclusion.

To this point, Anthropology was the focus of his work. In contrast, the next work was prepared for Marketing 131-N class. Dated June 30, 1976, it is an analysis of an actual businessman's marketing strategy with recommendations to improve his client base.

The book review format allows the student to read someone's work, think about it, and comment in response to a more general stimulus than the type posed by questions on an essay exam. The first book review is Dad's response to reading Dee Brown's *Bury My Heart at Wounded Knee*. He dated it March 11, 1974. It is interesting to note that his observations about the book address the author's style, structure and presentation, all elements of writing he would not even have considered prior to his experiences at college. In this essay, he begins to show an understanding of the stylistic use of elements of writing. The Instructor notes "perceptive". I agree.

Dad's response to reading C. W. Ceram's *Gods, Graves and Scholars* follows. Note that in the text he seems to identify Kurt March as the author. I have not been able to rectify this discrepancy. Next, *Monsieur Beaucaire* by Booth Tarkington, probably was an assigned reading; it was not something Dad would have selected for himself. After a brief recital of the main theme, Dad continues with a discussion of the role of the common man in the order of things citing, among others, Adam Smith, Isaac Newton, Voltaire, and Rousseau. Perhaps he had just finished a classical literature course. In his usual style, he manages to insert some personal examples to make his points, and ends with humor.

Dad's review of Robert Garner's The *Grafter's Handbook* in the course titled Principles of Horticulture must have been a dream come true. It combines an opportunity to study exactly what he entered college for, paired with an activity with which he was intimately familiar. His descriptive prose review is technical and concise. He foregoes both humor and personal experience for the opportunity to cram in every word possible detailing this – his - craft.

Late in 1979, a Ronald J. Glossop of Southern Illinois University at Edwardsville wrote a letter to Dad, who had inquired about two things. First he expressed interest in the Humanities Honors courses. Second, he suggested evening commuter courses. This letter is the university's response.

Finally, in June of 1980, Myron Stanley Nixon graduated from SIU-E with a degree in Anthropology. I attended that graduation and can attest from experience that as good as a parent can feel at seeing their child graduate, I felt even better as the child seeing my Father matriculate. Although she reportedly was there, I did not recognize the checkbook lady from the long black car.

Now 61 years old, he was in the autumn of his years but he had accomplished the three major goals of his life. First, as instilled by his Grandmother, he had acquired his own land which he had developed to a state where it supplied him and his family with the natural bounty that she held in such high esteem. Second, just as his mother had done before him, and perhaps in response to her example, he had raised his children successfully. Third, he had achieved his dream of becoming an Anthropologist and he didn't even have to ante up his right arm as he had offered to do. And, thanks to some reforming cannibals, he still had his left one too.

My sister recalls those days that he spent sitting in the swing under that great oak that he had nurtured back to health, in his "office", whittling bells and whistles and rolling pins and wooden chains as he waited for the next customer who wanted some blackberries or cherries or whatever he advertised on a homemade sign along the street near the mail box. I, too, can see him in these autumnal years of his life, cracking nuts in the garage while watching the sun set over his "north 40", the yellow leaves falling contentedly from his hybrid nut trees, children in graduate school and meaningful positions, diploma in hand, Grandmother in mind, turning to look back at what he had wrought and feeling good about his accomplishments. Autumn's Anthropologist!

With one degree complete (A. A. December 1976, L&C College) and now a second in hand (B. S., March 1980, SIU-E), Dad prepared to leave the university. Putting his now developed writing skills to work, he drafted a more serious prose piece called simply *Education*. It is not dated but from references within the text, it was prepared about 1980, or around the time of his graduation. In it, he looks back over a seven year period of his life of which he could understandably be proud. This document stands as an overall summary of his feelings about education, and, without benefit of humor, comprises his "senior thesis" in which his philosophy of adult education is presented. This work does as much as any other to aid in understanding the things that motivated him.

The version of this paper presented here I found as seven hand written pages complete with erasures, strikeouts, and other corrections – straight from his writing desk! Although the finalized version was never located, I trust this draft will successfully convey his message.

The Speech (1972)

by
Myron S. Nixon
(1972)

I was fifty-three. My children were grown and graduated from college. I was all set. Right where I had planned to be twenty years ago.

There was, however, this wild fleeting notion banging around in my head. I has[d] always wanted to go to college. I decided to try it. Why not? At least I could go until I flunked out.

A few weeks later I was enrolled at Lewis and Clark Community College, Godfrey, Illinois. I had been to a few classes and was going as strong as horseradish. My classes were at night. I worked six days a week for the Postal Department as a rural carrier.

In my speech class, each student was required to make several speeches-- all before his or her classmates. My first speech was to be an "explanatory" speech. I had decided to explain the culture, origin, history, and merits of the "Mitchell Heartnut". I gave each of my classmates several of the nuts I had grown and explained about them.

Arriving at my next speech class the following week, I parked as usual, locked my car, and started across the parking lot toward my classroom. I then heard someone calling my name and glancing around I noticed a lady sitting behind the wheel of a long black car. She asked me to come to her car. I did so. She then asked me if my name was Myron Nixon. I readily admitted that much and made a mental note to admit nothing more. She held up one of the Mitchell Heartnuts and said that it had been given to her by her granddaughter, a classmate of mine.

Then she came directly to the point and said "Mr. Nixon, I like the flavor of this nut, the way it cracked out, and everything about it. I want a bushel of them. How soon can you deliver them and how much will they cost"? She had her checkbook in one hand and a pen in another.

I could see this lady had her tail curled and really meant business, and I longed to hear that pen of hers scratch on that checkbook!

But alas! It wasn't to be. I explained to her "Madam, I am sorry I can't let you have a bushel of these nuts".

She tried again, "Mr. Nixon, would you please explain to me why you won't let me have a bushel of these nuts. Are you just being obstinate? I'll pay you".

"I'm sure you would, Madam, but a bushel of these nuts just does not exist. They are hybrid nuts--a result of cross breeding. I have only one bearing-age tree. I am somewhat of an amateur plant hybridizer and have enrolled here hoping to study genetics so I can pursue my hobby further".

She gave up then. I could see her face fall as she grudgingly thanked me and prepared to leave. It was then that I began to feel a little sorry for her. People with money seldom run into a situation where money won't do things for them, and when that happens, they become disgusted. Much the same, I imagine, as poor people do for lack of resources.

I re-opened conversation with her then, and said, "Madam, it really tears me up because I can't supply those nuts, Believe me, I would love to do so and nothing would please me more than to hear that pen scratch on the checkbook"!

This caused her to smile a little, and I thought I heard her mumble something that sounded a little bit like "Mercenary S. O. B.". I ignored what I thought I heard and continued with "I'll make a deal with you. Ill bring you a couple of grafted trees of this particular variety, plant them for you, and guarantee them to leaf out one year later, All this for twenty dollars per tree".

She hesitated a moment, then said "How long before they bear"?

Between six and ten years".

"My God man, I'm almost 49, I'll be 59 before they bear"!

"How old will you be in ten years if you don't plant the trees"?"

"All right, smart alec, you've got a deal".

Now it was my turn to be disgusted. I was half hour late for class. I should have had sense enough to run away and hide when I first saw her! I vowed to do just that if it should happen again.

After planting her trees the following spring, I also top-worked two small seedling black walnuts to Mitchell Heartnut. One of them bore two nuts the second year from the graft--sure made her happy.

My graduation from Lewis and Clark was in June 1977. I then transferred to Southern Illinois University at Edwardsville, Illinois, graduating in June, 1980. The lady appeared both times. At the last one, she had several friends with her. I couldn't imagine why anyone would attend graduation ceremonies of a total stranger. I soon found out. They all had grafting jobs they wanted me to do.

It seems that there should be some sort of a moral lesson here somewhere, but I can't seem to put my finger on it. Perhaps:

> "Just take it in stride
> Don't run off and hide
> It'll all come out in the end
> Everything will be right
> And we'll all take delight
> When we turn a stranger into a friend".

A Friend of My Friend

By
Myron Nixon

Odd and unusual things happen as we pursue our daily lives, often changing our lives completely.

I was fifty three when I decided to go to college. Obtaining a college degree was my lifelong ambition. The one thing I dreaded most was not being accepted by my younger classmates. This never happened. I attended classes at night and my classmates came out of the factories, grocery stores, etc. Just a bunch of old dummies like me. We got along wonderfully.

Each semester we were required to take courses in English, Grammar or Speech. We made our speeches before our classmates. And on this particular night I made a demonstration speech. I demonstrated the Throp Black Walnut. The Throp Black Walnut, when cracked, will yield its kernel whole and intact. At the end of my speech I gave everyone a hand full of the nuts.

Some days later a man came to my house, explained that he was a friend of one of my classmates and asked to see the Throp walnuts. We cracked a few of the nuts and when he left I gave him a pocket full of the nuts.

Some weeks later I began to hear stories of a fellow who went around to the taverns and made bets that he could crack a walnut and recover the kernel whole and intact.

Shortly thereafter he came back here and as he described himself, "a friend of my friend" and asked for a few more of those walnuts.

I obliged him but gave him some <u>different</u> walnuts. I have never seen him since! And it saddens me, and sort of hurts my feelings that my old friend of my friend never comes to visit me anymore.

Anthropology. October 9, 1973 (Examination)

MYRON NIXON

1. a.
Man is the end product, or summation of his environment and his heredity.

H + E = Homo

Solving this peculiar equation is much more difficult than merely writing it down. While anthropology gives us some insight into man's past, by providing us with skeletal remains and tools (to reveal some aspects of his bodily form and his culture), we are still left in the dark about the greater portion of Man's past. The medical profession rests almost wholly on one small invention, namely the microscope. Not so, anthropology. It is itself rests upon a very broad base which embraces nearly all of the known sciences. An early anthropologist, Britisher R. R. Morrett once declared, "Anthropology is History or it is nothing". I would emulate Morrett somewhat and say "anthropology is everything or it is nothing". Hastening to explain Anthropology is made up of people of science from all disciplines. Foremost among these I would place the Chemist, Biologist, Geologist and Mathematician. Next I would list the Climatologist, Geographer, Historian and Vulcanologist. The Archaeologist and the Ethnologist furnish us with physical proof also. Once while talking with Stuart Struever of recent Koster Site fame, I heard him say "I can use anyone who has an hour of spare time". Yes, Anthropology appears to be about everything. Now about the "Nothing". It is my opinion Anthropology without these other disciplines would indeed be nothing. We would be unable to seek out data about Mans' past and also unable to analyze any we happened to stumble onto.

1. b.
After much consideration I have purposely left out such words as:

Progress
Civilization
Evolution
survival
Fittest

I leave out the word "progress" because I am not at all sure we are progressing, or moving forward. With all our wars, pollution, etc., it seems very unlikely indeed. Civilization, Anthropologically speaking, refers to Agriculture, Public works, a Written Language and pertaining to a city. My own concept embraces much, much more. I would include some sort of kindness of mind and deed, some fellowship and good humor, and most of all pity for the weak, the sick, the deranged and the handicapped. The last three omitted words, Evolution, Survival and fittest. I seem to connect them in my mind with Darwin and his famous quote (Survival of the Fittest). It would seem to me this would make more sense if it were written "survival of the Survivalist". In other words we know that Man is the end product of Evolution, but not necessarily always the fittest. We are the product of who and what accidentally survives for any reason whatever.

[Grade, Part 1 = C]

2. a.
In order to gather data an archaeologist must first select a site. This can be done by aircraft, motor vehicle or even by boat. More often however, he simply legs it out. He first pokes around anywhere he can, questions the local people, and reads or re-reads any other reports of previous archaeologists that might exist. When he does decide he has a likely site he then must secure permission to dig as well as trespass, if his site happens to be on private property, then comes the enormous task of promoting funds, labor and any other things he may need. Should he get this far then must begin his survey. First a general survey of the general vicinity. The final survey would be a specific survey of the site, to divide it into six foot squares. Also a topographical survey would be included here. As he and his crew proceed, any artifacts, bones, etc. must be charted accurately. Should his dig be of sufficient magnitude to include laboratories on the site or close by, he would request all information be returned immediately to the site. This is of enormous importance and can be a great help to both the digger and the evaluator. This is known as "feedback".

b.
Ethnology a study of, and about living cultures tends to bring an altogether new concept into practice. The ethnographer seeks out primitive cultures, ghetto peoples, rural and suburban or city groups. In fact, he may study people anywhere under any conditions. He lives with his selected group, learns the language and measures them physically and in every way tries to ascertain their total way of life. His main assignment and intent is to study these people without interrupting or changing their way of life. I would think

his main obstacle would be religion in this case. It is important to know and understand the complexities of each group's religion because religion plays such an important role in the life of all people. Each set of superstitions being similar but different. Graphs and charts are the chief result of the ethnographers activities.

c.

Problems and pitfalls are many and varied for the Anthropologist. Money being one of the foremost. Competent labor and analysis is a constant problem. Religious superstition is an old nemesis also. Religion being merely a state of mind, or at best something that exists only in the mind and leaves very little in the way of proof for the anthropologist. Archaeologists and ethnographers must also decide to doctor or not doctor primitive people they may be working with, or living with. This leaves them wide open for any scorn or blame that may come especially from their decisions, regardless of what they do. Always leaving an opening for the second guess.

In summary, I must conclude an Anthropologist does not have an easy life, is underpaid, misunderstood, and often scorned, even by his own colleagues, but I would give my right arm to be one.

[Instr: Grade, Part 2 = A -; Overall Grade = B]

ANTH 231. November 5, 1973

Second Test - Take Home

THE QUESTION

1. Evolution can be defined as "the development of new life forms out of pre-existing forms." In class the following interrelated concepts were used to explain how evolution happens: adaptation, variation, natural selection, survival of the fittest, Romer's rule, gene pool, and mutation.

(a) Define each of these seven terms in your own words and then,
(b) Use them to describe how the evolutionary process occurs.

2, Describe six trends of physical change that appear in the fossil record (e. g. increase in brain size, reduction in snout, etc.) And explain how they are interrelated and inderdependent. Use diagrams to illustrate your discussion.

THE RESPONSE

Adaptation is a term used to describe how a given person, group, or tribe, reacts to a change in the environment, food procurement, climatic change, etc. any change, either sudden, or over a long span of time must be adapted to. Man is thought to be the most adaptable of all species.

[Instr comment: in evolution adapt doesn't refer necessarily to a tribe or a cultural group]

Variation is used to indicate differences within a species or group. Such as differences in hair and eye color, temperament, etc. Physical, mental and habitual traits vary considerably in all groups. This is the result partly of environmental differences and partly by heredity. The total gene pool has such a tremendous mathematical range that odds of two alike are nearly impossible.

Natural selection is the process by which certain individuals who have characters that help them to compensate to any given set of circumstances in their specific environment, tend to have more progeny that those less able to become adapted.

Survival of the fittest means the survival of the strongest, the smartest and the most adaptable [Instr comment = this term better - all inclusive]. General health would seem to be the key here, as the healthiest would tend to be stronger, live longer and be more active sexually, therefore leaving more and better progeny.

Romers Rule teaches us that changes, ever so small and slight are very hard to discern at the time, but adding them all up at the end of along period of time can make a tremendous difference. It seems to me one of the hardest words to understand for the Anthropology student is the simple little word "Million". Can anyone fully comprehend how much time a million years really is? [comment = good point!].

Gene pool is that specific amount of genes contained in a group that select mates and breed together. This is the total genetic information of both sexes.

Mutation is a term describing a sudden variation in plant or animal cells that is thought to be caused by mutilation or physical damage to a cell, such as to cause it to radically change. This is not to be confused with variation over a longer period of time. Radiation is known to cause mutants. Mutants reproduce themselves in daughter cells.

My concept of evolutionary process would be that life began from a single cell. This single cell divided and reproduced itself, and in so doing established the long, complicated and complex world of living plants and animals that we know today.

As these tiny one celled creatures became adapted to their particular environments changing conditions of climate, humidity and temperature caused some to die and others to become adapted to the new way of life. Variation and mutation had already began. Natural selection also played its role and selected certain variants to live and others to die out. Only the strong and healthy could survive and so these are the ones that left the most progeny. Survival of the Fittest is the term we use to designate this process.

Now by a multitude of small changes, we have something when we add them all up that often does not even resemble our original form, does not live in the same environment, and cannot live on the same food. This is Romers Rule in application.

As these various forms of life move away from their ancestral forms the tend to form groups, or a kind of a "Birds of a Feather" cult. Gene pools are formed and along with the slower variations within the group, mutation also occurs, to bring about change. New forms constantly evolve, some live, some die. Evolution is always at work, but never stopping.

[Instr: grade = A]

2. Physical changes appearing in the fossil record include:
    1. Changes in the pelvic structure from Quadruped to Man [original with hand drawn illustration]
    2. Skull balanced and centered on spine [drawings]
    3. Skull more rounded and greater capacity [with drawings of Australopithecus africanus and Modern Man].
    4. Mandible shorter and much lighter [drawings of Heidelburg Man and Modern Man]
    5. Teeth lighter and smaller [drawings]
    6. Jawbone wider in back in Modern Man [drawings Ape and Modern Man]

As Man evolved away from the ape, some very interesting changes were left in the fossil record. Positive proof of these changes can be found by Anthropologists in sedimentary rock.

The biggest step of all came when Man learned to walk upright. This freed his front feet for other duties. Among other things he used his hands for, was to put food into his mouth. When his pelvis broadened and became more bucket shaped this also influenced his spinal column and gave his spine somewhat of a double curve. His head then sat squarely upon his spine, more like an apple on a stick. By using his front feet to feed himself he no longer needed such a long snout, nor such a heavy lower jaw, nor his long ripping incisors. As his snout became shorter, his vision became more acute because his nose was no longer in the way. Bifocal [comment = stereoscopic] vision would, of course, be no advantage here unless his brain was capable of interpreting the message sent to it. So the brain also became larger and more adept. As the heavy brow ridge gave way to a more rounded, curved forehead, this also increased the size of his brain case, enabling man to become a better thinker and reasoner.

Once again we must return to Romers Rule and marvel at the changes that have brought man to his present position. So small, so slight, as to be almost indiscernible, yet over the long span of time when we add them all up we have Homo sapiens.

[Instr: grade part 2 = A-; overall grade = A]

Anthropology 232. Nov. 6, 1974 (Examination)

MYRON NIXON

1.

Postulates can be defined as that set of rules, or understandings, by which certain peoples, groups or cultures live. They consist of natural and/or geographical facts of the given locality, plus the nature of man himself within said boundaries.

The very nature of man interacting with his natural surroundings, and his total existence is known as existential postulates. Deep inner assumptions, or mental assumptions, are known to Anthropologists as Normative Postulates.

As an example I would refer to our own mountain states of Kentucky, Tennessee and the Carolinas. These simple people have a deep love for their rocky, timbered land, and are able to maintain themselves with their small garden patches and occasional hunting and gathering. This way of life I would define as the "existential".

In searching for the "normative" here I would point to their religions and other superstitions. They believe in moon signs, bear signs, and many, many more signs of good and bad that have no value to anyone except their own particular culture. I was astonished when a man explained to me that if he burned corn cobs in his fire to cook on or warm himself, this would cause his corn to burn up in the field the following season. He also believed making and selling whiskey was not necessarily serving the Lord, but he went to church, and even sang gospel songs regularly and had great hopes of going to heaven when he died.

[Instr: Grade = B-]

2.

Societies are made up of people, people are, of course, individuals. Individuals are exactly that, and each one different from any other. While individuals in a society are in many ways very similar, in fact their culture seems to be exact. It is not true, and herein lies the basis for cultural change, very slowly for sure, but change nevertheless.

As an example I would offer my own experiences as a boy. My father, a farmer died when I was a baby and I was raised in two distinct cultures. One set of grandparents of English ancestry, the other German. Each brought from N. Europe his own set of rules. One grandfather could, and would, with very little coaxing, dance a jig, sing a song and play the fiddle simultaneously. Very entertaining, indeed, if "Auch der Lieber Augustine" just happened to be your favorite tune. My English grandfather looked upon such a ritual as sacrilegious, even down right barbaric, by Jove! Two sets of cultures one half mile apart, however each had common ground with the other. They worked very well together and have now blended into one society, while manifest through the behavior of individual people, now have one culture, a new one.

[Instr: Grade =C]

3.
I do agree with the theory that societies with more ascribed statuses have fewer inner tensions than the societies with many achieved statuses.

I would refer back to the mountain people of Ky., Tenn. & the Carolinas. They have few achieved statuses and are known to be relatively free of the so-called stress-diseases. They also have few ascribed statuses also, for merely living is to them ample evidence of ascribed status.

Whatever status they possess, they are born with (ascribed). They have no deadlines, no time limits, and they are certainly are not trying to achieve the next higher job in their particular professions because there is no such step. If I thought it at all possible I would join them tomorrow.

[Instr: Grade = C+. Frown face with "Sad, not mad" and "Myron! What happened?"]

Anthropology. November 26, 1974, (Examination)

MYRON NIXON

1.

Australopithecus africanus was first found and named in 1916 by Raymond A. Dart, professor of anatomy at the University of Witwatersand, Johannesburg, S. Africa. The find consisted of a nearly perfect juvenile skull, face and teeth. Later in 1936 and thereafter more fossils were found at Sterkfountain, Mokapansgat, Lewarthens and Kromdrosai. So the foundation and part of the framework of our ancestors had been constructed. Professor Dart must have been a remarkable man indeed to have recognized the importance of his find, and to have diagnosed the situation so perfectly. It may be noted here that he did not name this fossil after himself or his colleagues. A bit of modesty that has not persisted since in Botany, Zoology or Marine Biology. Of the late discoveries, some very important information has been garnered. A. Africanus, even at this early date, had quite a number of Hominid adaptations. Notably the skull, pelvis, face and femur. Brain case of approximately 450 -700 cc, protruding jaw without chin, pelvis constructed so as to promote upright posture, alveolar arch rounded and short, much reduced length in canine teeth, teeth smaller and do not flare out or project. The femur bone fit the pelvis so as to promote uprightness.

Now our Southern Ape has not only the conformation of body required to walk upright and release his front legs to use as he wished. He was now ready to produce culture and was able to defend and feed himself. He did have culture and he did use tools.

Australopithecus robustus has also been found in these same Pleistocene beds, the best known perhaps is the discovery by Brown at Swartkans in 1948. A. robustus seems to be a larger bulkier and slower version of A. africanus. He seemed to not possess the vigor of A. africanus and did not persist as well in the fossil record.

Next came a somewhat controversial find by the Leakeys in Bed 1 of Olduvai gorge. Remains of several individuals of A. africanus, along with one A. robustus skull. By their slightly smaller teeth and cranial contours they are thought by some to be more hominized than A. africanus. More finds would help here. In any event, Homo habilis is the name given to this find.

The fossil called Pithecanthropus came to light in 1891 but was not accepted as Homo Erectus until 1930 when it was shown to be very much like Peking man found in a cave near Peking, China, called Choukoutein Locus I. Peking man had a larger cranial capacity, he had fire and better tools and weapons. A. africanus was finished by then. He had evolved out and left the groundwork for further advancement. Finds in Ternefine, Algeria and Heidelberg, Germany confirm this.

Seemingly next in line would be Heidelberg Man found in lower Pleistocene gravel at Mawr, near Heidelberg, Germany. Only one fossil has been found and the jaw seems to be Home erectus with dentition somewhat more evolved or advanced.

Next in line we come to the so called Swanscombe skull found near Steinbrim England, also the Soutechenade specimens found in southwestern France. Cranial capacities were around 1460-1470 cc which is very near average for Modern Man.

Next came the most interesting Neandertal finds, the first in a valley near Dusseldorf, Germany in 1865. Two more finds at Spy, Belgium, helped consolidate our knowledge, then many more from France, Spain, Palestine and North Africa. Perhaps diversity is the most predominant of Neandertal characteristics and "Diverse" we are. Now we are saddled with the problem of dissecting and naming our many so called races. A task that seems hopeless. In any event we are now called by taxonomists Homo sapiens sapiens. Wonder what it will be tomorrow?

[Instr: Grade = C. Comments: "relation of Neandertal to us?"]

Theory or evidence? First we must have some concrete facts, something we can be firm about. Evidence is always the basis for theory. Without something to tie to, our theory will be no more than wisps of smoke floating in the breeze. Often extremely meager evidence can produce remarkably good theory. In archaeology, the bones, the site, the artifacts, anything physical is evidence. Our theory of what happened here must conform to the physical evidence. It must also meet the ravages of "TIME". Therefore, we must often change or modify our theory as we go, or in other words, revise it to fit any new evidence.

My most exasperating moment in Anthropological theory came when I read the story "The Naked Ape". This non theorized man had lost his hair because he ran so fast he needed to be hairless in order to let his body heat escape. He failed to mention the cat, deer, wolf, rabbit, in fact any other mammal that man might chase or run away from, retained its body hair. This, in my opinion, is poor theoretical thinking.

[Instr: Grade = none. Comments: "Good point".]

Taxon, Nomenclature. Sign, Mark, Name, Number. Any of the above words we use to describe or designate something, is of course, not as good as the article itself. Obviously we can't always point to our house every time we designate it, nor can we carry it around with us for that purpose. So we refer to it in speech, as the old house, or my old shack.

In the field of evolution we encounter in the fossil record many aspects of very nearly the same fossil. Almost, but not quite. Therefore, in order to keep them straight we must find names and the names must be readily available for use. They must be specific, and refer to one, and only one, form.

Admittedly this is not a perfect system but it is, in my belief, the best we have. And I believe the scientific world would readily adopt a better system should someone come up with one.

Names are fleeting, at best merely symbolism, bones, fossils and physical evidence is the real meat of Archaeology.

[Instr: Grade = A-. Overall grade = B/B-. Comments: evolution is a continuous line of change. Names arbitrarily divide sets into categories.]

Anthropology. May 6, 1974, (Examination)

Rites of Passage

Transitions rites, commonly known as rites of passage, play a very important role in the lives of the people concerned. While literally dozens of such rites mark a person's life, the most often used are, Birth, Adolescence, Marriage and Death. This, of course, gives us two major classifications. Those affecting the entire group or community, and those affecting everyone <u>but</u> the individual involved. Birth and Death obviously has no conscious effect on the individual involved. Adolescence rites have a mental impact on the individual. Such rites range from puberty rites and circumcision, to graduating from Junior High or Eighth Grade. Completing these rites gives the individual the sense of achievement or "over the hump" feeling and he may look forward to the next step in his growing up.

Marriage rites are also rites participated in by whole groups of social societies. Usually the Mother of the Bride tends to the formalities. In short she proclaims to everyone in sight, sound or hearing that her daughter is to be married upon a certain day, at a certain hour, at a certain place, by a certain priest, etc. this also serves the community to the extent that it gives a subtle warning to any and all of her daughters past competitors. They are not to try any more of their sexual wiles on Joe Blow. Also from now on should they try to become pregnant by Joe Blow they would have no recourse to any law of paternity, because Joe Blow is already taken. [Instr: you mean in US]

Birth rites take many forms, the most common naming and baptism. This rite is for the benefit of the group only and serves merely as an announcement that a child is born, his name is Joe and he has been duly baptized. [Instr: sets up their relationship and responsibilities to new members socially].

Death rites are participated in by the whole community and are held solely by and for the living. This is usually a chance to impress others. In fact, the last chance. The living relatives are now being judged by their friends and neighbors. The casket price, the resplendency of attire, size and quality of the grave marker, selection of cemetery, etc.

So, to sum it all up it is my opinion that transition rites are all a bunch of baloney. On the other hand life would be dull indeed without them, and both the individual and the community derive great benefit from them, both mental and physical. They help us while away the time, and give us food and gossip, and help us perpetuate our culture. In fact, they tend to insure our culture will persist into the future.

[Instr: B/B-]

Marriage

Marriage is that time in life that two people choose, as they set out to further civilization. It is so common and yet so complicated, so easy to understand and yet so complex, that it is truly surprising that it ever works out. Every living thing is involved here, every bird, animal, fish and insect at a given point in time will, build a nest, mate, and raise young. It is so natural we tend to overlook its magnitude. Without the Instinct, Sexual Drive, Imprint, and perhaps a couple dozen other words used by our Scientific people, it seems reasonably certain Man would have gone the way of the Dodo and passenger pigeon.

It would seem to me that we are all born with Imprint patterns and as our life unfolds, we need not wonder what to do next, we merely have the next move revealed to us, and proceed smoothly on our way. I'm sure if young people were aware of all the social obligations and responsibilities along with the multitude of other pit falls that awaited them, no amount of physical sexual drive could persuade them to start down the path of Marriage.

Yes, Marriage is much more than legalized or ceremonialized mating. Especially in America where we are free to choose at will our own mate for life. I believe sexually romantic love is at its best, and free for everyone in the U. S. A. I believe that Romantic love and Marriage is entered into for one reason alone. Physical Attraction and Sexual Desire. All the social niceties, and complexities come later, and are so secondary in nature that they need no further discussion.

[Instr: But what about cultures where marriages take place for other primary reasons? Why are they different in this respect? Incomplete. C- C+. Course Grade: B]

Marketing 131-N. June 30, 1976 (Mr. Krause)

MYRON NIXON

After meeting and talking with Mr. Mike Roa, it is my opinion that to increase his restaurant business he must locate new customers. He must educate and reeducate the public.

One area to be exploited could be the Spanish language classes at the local high schools and colleges. His ability to speak Spanish could be capitalized on and made into an asset. I would suggest the first target to be the adult classes at the local college. Night classes preferably. Many students here are studying Spanish because they plan future visits to Mexico, Central America or the Caribbean area. They will be delighted to meet Mr. Roa. He should invite them to visit his establishment, try his food and practice their Spanish on him and his waitress. He could even give each student a coupon worth 25¢ when used at his restaurant. On the back of this coupon he should have his name, address and location, perhaps a date and some means of identification so that he could make use of the information gained here for future targets in this area.

Mr. Roa is a personable, affable man. He appeared before our class clean and neat. He will have no trouble selling himself. I would be glad to introduce Mr. Roa to my Spanish teacher and her class, or help him in any other way I can.

Anthropology. Book Report, Mar 11, 1974

Bury My Heart at Wounded Knee by Dee Brown

This book impressed me as no other book of Indian lore has in the past. A book about Indians written by an Indian. The downright simplicity of this book is a mastery of style and research.

Perhaps one should keep in mind that Indians learned deceit and intrigue from the White Man along with English grammar and journalism. Dee Brown uses all of these in his book. He even had presence of mind and forethought enough to skim through the battle of the bighorn, the very thing White People would like to hear more about. This, of course, comes out in yet another book to be written later. More books, more money.

The story of Indian suffering and privation here is without a shadow of a doubt, true. No point or counterpoint is even debatable. He has presented it to us in such a masterful style and such simple verbiage that even the smaller points can easily be authenticated after a hundred years have past.

His white education shows through in a few instances. He is able to capture the sympathy of his readers at some points exactly as white authors do. He simply turns an Indian massacre of Whites into a justifiable crime, much the same way White authors uphold and justify massacres of Indians.

The fact comes home clear and concise. Indians were unable to cope with White people because they could not understand the treachery involved. It has ever been so. All over the world, the Man with the technology and the conniving mind to accompany it, have overrun and enslaved other peoples. I see no end in sight.

At this particular point in time it is hard to imagine the reason or reasons that Indians did not band together against the common enemy, the White Man. This history is repeating itself at present in both Africa and S. America.

[Instr: Grade = none. Comment = good report. To point and perceptive.]

Anthropology. Book Report, March 26, 1974

Gods, Graves and Scholars
C. W. Ceram

This book has caused me no end of indecision. Having read other books by Kurt March, this one seems to be away his usual style. When he launched into his praise of Heinrich Schleiman for his work in finding and excavating the City of Troy, I immediately thought this was just one German blowing up another. Other accounts of Schlieman at Troy I have read, relegate Schleiman to nothing much but a pot hunter and a destroyer of evidence. Later March has equal praise for Englishmen, Frenchmen, and even the Italian thief and pot hunter, Belzoni.

Now after some doubts I am ready to give March credit for being honest enough to give credit to anyone he believes to have served Anthropology and Archaeology well. I can hardly find fault with him because I know so little about the subject matter he is discussing.

The author's talent and mastery of Journalism is very apparent in the way he builds up his characters such as Mosley, Kaldwwey and Smith. Even more obscure workers in Anthropology and Archaeology are blown up and let down, almost at will. On occasion he starts out chapters with such a build up, never mentioning even the name of the person until several paragraphs have been written. Then dropping the name in sort of a bomb shell technique. He is equally talented at building up a certain site, or dig. I can't help but wonder why these same tactics wouldn't be of great advantage in our schools. I would certainly relieve some of the pangs of dullness, and dryness in Ancient and Modern History, and many other studies.

This is, in my opinion, a very good book, very well written and very thoroughly researched.

[Instr: Grade = none. Comments: "Many anthropologists react to him with your kind of indecision".]

HUMN 132. Semester Project

Discussion of a Historical or Biographical Novel
TITLE: *Monsieur Beaucaire*
AUTHOR: Booth Tarkington

A DISCUSSION OF MONSIEUR BEAUCAIRE

Prince Louis Phillippe de Valois, a young French nobleman who had been matched for betrothal by King Louis XV with a certain Lady of France, disguised himself as Monsieur Beaucaire, a barber in the service of the French envoy to Britain. In this guise he traveled to England, hoping to stall for time until Louis XV's wrath against him had cooled. Louis XV was much displeased that his order to marry had not been heeded by the young Prince.

In order to amuse himself, the young prince gambled with the noblemen of Britain. During one such gambling session he caught the Duke of Winterset with a card in his sleeve. He threatened to expose the Duke as a card cheat. In order to insure himself of the Frenchman's silence, the Duke of Winterset allowed himself to be blackmailed into introducing the young Frenchman to Britain's Lady Mary Carlisle. He is introduced by the young Frenchman to Lady Mary Carlisle as the Duke of Chateaurien.

With a great display of grace and good manners, the "Duke of Chateaurien" soon won favor with Lady Mary and he quickly became her most preferred suitor, even surpassing Winterset himself. En route home after a party one evening Winterset hired a band of ruffians to attack the young Frenchman. The "Duke of Chateaurien", of course, fought them bravely and valiantly, and, after being severely wounded in the ensuing melee, was rescued by his personal bodyguard. Winterset then denounced the young Frenchman as a low born imposter.

Lady Mary would have no more to do with him then, thinking him to be a low born despicable barber. Later he appeared at a party where his true identity was established and where, with much gusto, he denounced Winterset as a card cheat. Lady Mary was then ready to make amends, but the young Frenchman had changed his mind, and he had decided to return to France and marry the woman Louis XV had previously selected for him.

Eighteenth century England was not a good time for the common man to live and enjoy life. He was constantly subjected to higher taxes and longer working hours. The landed gentry were broke. They demanded more production from the land, so they could spend more time and money dilly-dallying around the courts, chasing dragons, and seeking honor.

The peasant class could not produce more from the soil. They could hardly maintain themselves. Young men were leaving the farms, because city life looked better. The Industrial Revolution had began, and labor was needed in the shops and in the factories. The low born common man, for once in his life, had a choice -- starve on the farm, or starve in the factory.

At this particular time in history (1710 - 1780) the winds of change were blowing across both Britain and Northern Europe. Adam Smith was putting together his principles of capitalism and economics. This theory soon became knows as Mercantilism. Isaac Newton had brought out his theory of gravitation and his great talent in mathematics had greatly shocked the whole of Europe. James Watt invented the steam engine in 1765, and it became apparent that such a device would change the whole economy. Voltaire was expressing his cynicism and doubting nature in literature, and seemed to be influencing others to doubt the establishment also. Chardin was in revolt himself for he persisted in painting material things and the humblest of people. His "Kitchen Maid," was one of his best works, and he became known to his fellow artists as the "Common Man." J. J. Rousseau (1712-1778) astonished the world with his theory that all men were born good, that all nature was good, and, therefore all men as things in nature were also good. He admired the "Noble Savages" whom he imagined were all upstanding men and women; this was quite a shocking idea during that particular time in history.

Little by little, the common man was receiving more respect, and he was even becoming the object of admiration by some. It became apparent that common-born men were not all devoid of talent and/or intelligence. The great class distinction, however, was to last another century or more; however, the winds of change were at least blowing–ever so gently, but blowing.

The young Frenchman, Prince Phillippe, while masquerading as a commoner, implored Lady Mary to accept him as a common man, an honest man, a man of good character and ability. She, of course turned him down, not wishing to compromise the training and beliefs she had held since childhood. The world called for titles, not names; a name without a title was nothing.

Today, two hundred years later, we can excuse her for her lack of prudence and insight. After all, she was English, and the English were not noted for the virtues of prudence and insight. They were noted for other virtues: stubbornness, stuffiness, and stoic dullness. Even today as one travels in Britain or in the colonies, one is constantly astonished by the great amount of class mindedness. One lady in New Zealand told me in no uncertain terms "Yank, I believe in crowned 'eads'".

Another time in Australia an elderly gentleman informed me "By Jove, Yank, the whole bloomin country 'as gone to ell'. We need a restoration of the class system."

The struggle against class distinction had barely begun in Britain; however, across the channel in France it was well under way. Monsieur Beaucaire gave us a hint of conditions in France when he tells us of his own plight. King Louis XV had selected a mate for him, and he left the country because he did not want to marry her. He wanted to select his own wife and would not submit to having his decisions and his life dictated by Louis XV.

Monsieur Beaucaire gives the reader an insight into actual conditions in France, not only among the nobility, but also among the common people. He was thinking for himself and would not allow the king to do the thinking for him, especially in such a personal matter as marriage. Mate selection by parents was a common practice both in Europe and Britain in this era; however, as Monsieur Beauciare illustrates, certain people were beginning to rebel against this tradition.

Monsieur Beaucaire's rebellion against old traditions represents and parallels the secret rebellion by the commoners against class distinctions. The common people of France were greatly exploited and overtaxed by the nobility. Furthermore, the French commoner was unable to support himself and his family. Young men had flocked from the farms to the factories seeking a better life.

Schooling was almost nonexistent among the common people; education was out of the question for them. Unemployment was rampant. Even the clergy were turning down aspiring young priests. Such dire conditions caused the common people to whisper dissatisfaction among themselves and to anticipate furtive rebellion.

Will man ever be free of class distinction? Will all men ever live without hunger? My answers to these questions would have to be a resounding "No." However I do think man can and will be as free as his mind permits him to be. Distribution of wealth in the world would be impossible to attain. The logistics of such a project would be insurmountable. So why not think we are all free, and rich, and hunger can never overtake us. I once read somewhere of a great lady, a queen, in fact, who, when informed that her subjects had no bread, replied "Let them eat cake". She lost her head in the deal.

Principles of Horticulture. October 4, 1976, Mr. Greenwood

In Robert Garners book, "The Grafter's Handbook", Chapter VIII deals with re-grafting, or changing existing trees.

<u>Topworking</u>

Much of the main branch of the tree is re-moved and scions of a desired variety are inserted into the cut ends of the main limbs. This work is done in the spring so as to take advantage of the imminent growing season. In preparing a tree for top-working you should keep in mind that large wounds are hard to heal. It is much better to make several smaller wounds than one large one. I try never to cut a limb larger than two inches in diameter.

<u>Frameworking</u>

Frameworking is similar to topworking, however, there are some important advantages. Frameworked trees will yield large crops much quicker than top-worked trees. They also remain healthy in situations where topworked trees may die. In situations where bark canker is prevalent frameworking is advantageous. In frameworking the large limbs are cut back about halfway and new shoots are instilled every few inches directly into the limb. In about three years all the existing laterals are removed and new varieties are installed all along the existing limb.

Bridge grafting, inarching and approach grafting are also used on mature trees, usually to save existing trees damaged or girdled by rodents, implements or cancer.

Chapt IX
Conclusion

The final chapter of Robert Garners great book, "The Grafter's Handbook", is one of the most interesting I have ever read. This concluding chapter deals with:

1. Stock/Scion interaction
2. Graft Hybrids, Chimeras and Specific Influence

3. Grafting as an aid to the investigator
4. Invention of Grafts.

Mr. Garner explains stock/scion interactions, the effect of stock on scion, and scion on stock. This is a subject of great complexity, very seldom discussed among men of Horticulture. Graft hybrids and chimeras are treated in much the same way. Mr. Garner is absolutely frank with his readers when he says hybridization cannot result from grafting. He rightly dubs this superstition. Chimeras he explains are merely plants having intermixed or overlaid tissues. In his three paragraphs on Grafting as an aid to the Investigator, Mr. Garner points out grafting is increasingly employed in plant hormone and propagation studies. We also know apples and cherries are tested to see if they have virus diseases by merely grafting them onto wild crab apple or wild cherry. If the virus is present in the scion, it causes death in the rootstock within thirty days. In his remarks on the invention of grafts, or perhaps the patenting of procedure, is pertinence in itself. Nothing is new. It probably has been done before. He quotes Sir Francis Drake of Oxford in 1672: "Other variations I have purposely omitted so that from these an ingenious lover of this art will re-discover them, and further his pleasure and contentment".

Correspondence. Ronald J. Glossop November 14, 1979

From School of Humanities, SIU Edwardsville to Myron Nixon

Dear Mr. Nixon:

Thank you for writing to me in response to our invitation to enroll in our Humanities Honors courses. My congratulations to you for going back to school at age 53 and for sticking with the effort so that you will soon graduate from S. I. U. E.

I especially appreciate your calling my attention to the desirability of scheduling a course at night once a week for people who do not live close to campus. As a matter of fact, we have a course scheduled that way for Spring Quarter, Baseball and the American Novel taught by Professor Paul Gaston on Tuesday evenings. (See the enclosed sheet.) I hope that this course is one that would appeal to you.

It was good to hear from you. Perhaps I will see you sometime, at your graduation if not before.

Sincerely;

Ronald J. Glossop

Education

[by
Myron S. Nixon]

Webster's New World Dictionary defines education; the process of training and developing the knowledge, skill, mind, character, etc., by formal schooling; teaching; training. It may be safely assumed that anything we learn during the course of our entire lifetime may be considered education. It may also be reasonably assumed that our minds are more receptive to learning at certain times during our lifetime. When are these times?

It has been our custom to start children into schools at the age of five or six years old, and keep them in school for the next twelve to twenty years. It seems logical to educate our children during the early years of their lives so that they can then use their education to further their economic positions during the remaining years of their lives. Sounds good. But does it work?

In some cases it works perfectly, in others it is a dismal failure. We seem to overlook the fact that all children are not alike. No two are identical. The educable period or periods in one person's life may not coincide with those of another, in fact, seldom does.

With this in mind, and the results of our efforts painfully apparent to us, it may be a good idea to take a long, second look, at our efforts in the field of education. Somewhere along the line between 1940 and 1970 adult education came into being. Adult education has grown by leaps and bounds and is still growing. Why has adult education become so successful? The answer is so simple it seems we should have known it all along. Adults are going back to school because they want to. The adult student one encounters on the college campus is there because his mental attitude is receptable to education. He usually has a definite idea of what he wants in education and he pursues his goal relentlessly. He also enjoys himself immensely.

Adult students come from all walks of life. They come from the factory and study electricity, management, and labor relations. They come from the stores and study business, personnel management and accounting. They come from public works projects and study political science, speech and mass communications. I have talked to many of these people on the campus of Lewis and Clark College and the campus of Southern Illinois University,

Edwardsville. They do well in classes, have good grades and are respected by their teachers and fellow students.

Probably the most rewarding facet of all this is the rewards they receive from their employers. They receive advances in pay in accordance with their achievements in various levels of education. They receive advancement and promotion in their jobs. Many move on to better paying jobs elsewhere, others remain in their original job, often moving up the ladder in their particular firm.

Another great advantage could be easily overlooked. All of these people have made a better life for themselves, but look what a great boon this is to the community. What an enrichment has come to the entire community, and the country. Education is the life blood of our economy. Better educated people demand better economic conditions. If we are to maintain our position of leadership in world affairs we cannot afford to waste even one small portion of the ability of our people.

I think SIUE and the community colleges of this area are to be congratulated for their efforts to enrich this great industrial area. I readily admit that I was one of the detractors when SIUE was established, and when the State of Illinois bought the Old Monticello College. I am ashamed to admit that I was one of those who growled and bitched about the great waste of my tax money by the state, when these schools were established. I am grateful that someone had the foresight and perseverance to proceed with these educational projects in the face of mounting criticism.

One might ask; why don't more adults return to school? Why don't more of our adult population take advantage of the opportunities offered by the new colleges in our local community? There are several reasons. Foremost is the awful lurking suspicion that one may flunk out and become the laughing stock of the group at work or at home. This would be a tremendous loss of prestige. It may even bring shame upon a whole family. I know of no way we can overcome this fear and entice more adults back to school, because it is a reality. Anyone may flunk.

The second greatest reason why adults fear returning to school is merely a hallucination, and has no substance whatever. This reason deals with acceptance. Adults fear they will be out of place and will not be accepted by the other students. They think the other students will look upon them as some sort of oddity. Nothing could be further from the truth. In fact, the night classes consist mostly of adult students. I often look around me and wonder how such a fear could have ever entered my mind.

Another barrier adult students encounter that may prevent them from re-entering college is purely economical. The actual cost of education in money is stupendous. Tuition has increased rapidly along with books and transportation. Many adults have a feeling of guilt when they spend money for education, money they think could better be used elsewhere.

Scholarships, grants, and fellowships can be obtained easily but few people know how or where to apply for financial aid. It is only after one has attended college for some time that he may learn of the many ways he may obtain financial aid for education. Why the general public is not aware of this, I don't know. I suppose people don't bother to look into financial aid unless they are desperate for funds to keep their children in school.

Time enters the picture also when adults think of going back to college. Most people without a college education are obligated to work long hours. Often the only time an adult can spare for classes is at night, and he may be required to give up most of his social life in order to attend his night courses. Many of us also work shift work in factories. Consequently we may change shifts each week and would be unable to attend even night courses regularly. Recently I heard the Vice-President of SIUE mention that the University was contemplating a weekend schedule where adult students may attend classes on Friday, Saturday and Sunday. This seems like a remarkably astute plan and I hope to see it get underway soon. I think it would go far toward creating more opportunity for the adult student.

SIUE appears to be in an ideal location to serve the great industrial complex surrounding it. This is the very heart of industrial central Illinois. It is located also in an appropriate location to serve agricultural central Illinois. I have talked with students within a radius of fifty miles in all directions including St. Louis and rural areas to the west and north of St. Louis.

I particularly like the structure of curriculum at SIUE. General Studies is the backbone of education, and I think students learn more and have a broader scope of general education during the two years of General Studies than after they declare a major and begin to specialize.

Both Lewis & Clark and SIUE use the old method of teaching. I refer here to the so called regurgitation system, whereby the student swallows information from textbooks and lectures and later regurgitates this information at exam time. I don't mean to knock the system because it has served us well in the past, and I really don't know of a better system. Some classes I have attended recently at SIUE have changed the format altogether and grades are assigned to the student by the use of other means, usually by writing papers on selected topics.

Instructors at Lewis and Clark and SIUE are well informed and very conscientious about their work. I have never encountered a poor teacher. It gives me great satisfaction to have been a college student under Instructors as dedicated as those that I have had the privilege to study under.

In summary, I have enjoyed every moment of my college life. My classmates have been wonderful. One can't help but learn under such circumstances. I shall be reluctant to graduate and leave such a pleasant experience behind me.

VIII. TOO SOON WE ARE OLD (1980-2000)

At age 61, Dad was a diploma bearing Anthropologist. He had his own house and property; he enjoyed a good reputation in the community and the region for his work in plant genetics. He joked that he had served as 'President Nixon' of NAFEX but that he wasn't crooked. His education complete and his political career over, he was ready to settle into his mature years.

His writing at this point became recreational, much as it had been before he began his seven year adventure in higher education. No more term papers or book reports; no more exams or essays; no more Instructors to grade his work. He now could write what and when he wanted. Although he regretted leaving school and its - by his own admission - unanticipated rewards, his course work and term papers were behind him. He now was prepared to create on his own and at his own pace.

Two pieces above that he wrote during this period included *At the Clinic/At the Hospital* (August 10, 1989) and *The Left Handed Cannibal* (July 31, 1997). Another work came from an unanticipated source. In 1989-1990 my wife and I had moved back to Illinois. While living in Springfield, we negotiated a fair sized contract with Commonwealth Edison of Chicago to complete an archaeological survey of approximately 3,600± acres of their property. As fee simple owners, they proposed to sell the land at public auction and the state required them to complete, among other items, an archaeological assessment prior to transfer of the land. We offered to do the work and to prepare a report detailing the results of our investigations. Situated in Christian and Sangamon counties, the proposed land sale tracts were just south of Springfield, the state capitol.

In earlier times, Midwestern farmers worked their land by hand, using their strength, will, determination, animals, and their children. In those days there was no agricultural advantage to owning large tracts of land. Even with all the support he could muster, a single farmer could only work so many acres and anything beyond that was excess. Unless rented, it might lie fallow.

Property lines were less fluid then than they are now, family homestead boundaries often remaining in place across generations. Various devices marked the boundaries between your land and your neighbor's. "Corner stones", sometimes keyed into the township/range land grid, marked some property limits. Linear boundaries were equally as often traced with a living stand of a plant called the hedge, hence the "hedgerow". In addition to separating property boundaries, these hedgerows kept livestock away from growing crops, thereby protecting the fall harvest.

The elders constructed these living barriers by planting Osage orange trees next to each other and bending them over in their juvenile stages of growth, thus creating 'hog tight' property and field boundaries. Property owners called this process "laying hedge" and some individuals specialized in creating these living boundary markers.

With agricultural mechanization, the concept of boundaries changed. From about 1940 forward, new equipment allowed extension of the individual farmer's effort by allowing one man to cultivate more acreage than before. Consolidation of land became more common. With these changes in property lines, many owners simply forgot about many of the corner stone locations, but the living hedges, although now functionally obsolete, still grew along many old property lines.

At the time we undertook to survey Edison's holdings around Sangchris Lake, many of the small farms in Christian and Sangamon counties located beyond Edison's holdings had already been bought and consolidated into larger, more modern farmsteads. Landowners interested in longer field rows as a means to improve cultivation efficiency gradually removed the old property markers to create continuously cultivated fields, uninterrupted by barriers, and more conducive to heavy farm equipment of today.

Land renters, like the farmers on the lands owned by Edison, were less motivated to make such improvements to property that they did not own and so, when we undertook the survey of Edison owned lands, several examples of the old hedgerow property boundaries remained in place.

The 1998 archaeological field crew, mostly from urban Springfield and with no background on a farm, noted these geometrically aligned remnant hedgerows, wondering what they were and why they were there. Remembering hedgerows as a boy, it occurred to me to ask Dad about them and their use, propagation, growth and management as property barriers. I thought it might make an interesting appendix to the report that we had agreed to prepare for Commonwealth Edison.

Well, he reasoned, as a credentialed Anthropologist it behooved him to take on this assignment as his first job. He was delighted with the opportunity to put his newly won degree to work. He took it on with a vengeance. Written in 1990, the essay below titled *Hedge* harked back to an earlier time when the hedge was a common feature of the agricultural landscape, written, of course, by an Anthropologist (M. Nixon 1998.).

Another work, *The Quick Change*, is a short essay dated April 15, 1997, that recalls Dad's appreciation of family ties that is apparent in his earlier works, with one exception. While the earlier works are through his eyes as a child, this piece is through his adult eyes. Identical in both scenarios, however, is the deep and genuine affection characteristic of his sense of family. This, no doubt, was an artifact of his relationship with his Mother and Grandmother, expressed in America, as a remnant memory of an earlier European heritage.

Proving that an education does not blunt a sense of humor, *The Cake*, dated May 2, 1997, relates the story of a treat that Mom made for some sort of a local social affair. The cake, decorated with prized walnuts, is mysteriously vandalized before it reaches the table. Finding proof in circumstantial evidence, Dad reconstructs the crime and identifies the villain through unconventional means. CSI Chesterfield!

Written on July 26, 1997, *Reading the Alton Telegraph* is a prose discussion of a common complaint about the popular but admittedly messy local paper. Although this appears to be a letter to the editor type of work, I do not know if Dad ever submitted it to the Telegraph, or, if he did, if they ever published it. Or if they published it, whether acted upon by its addressee, the Editor.

The next piece, *Thomas* (dated January 1998), relates a prank pure and simple. It establishes an improbable relationship between Dad and a tomcat, in which Dad portrays himself as the victor in a battle of wits with that cat. As often is the case, it is not clear if this story relates an actual event or not, a stylistic element that Dad often used to entertain his audience. It shows the prankster side of him, but, whether true or not, it also shows the mature construction of a trained writer. It is an example of a sense of humor surviving even the most serious cadre of serial academic editors called in nice words, Instructors.

Dad often portrayed the cat as a prankster, whether by the creature's own volition or not. Another piece, titled *The Smart Cat*, exemplifies the role of the feline in society as he perceived it.

The desk where Dad wrote was in the front room of the Chesterfield home on the right side of the room as you walked in the front door (the earlier dinosaur bone room). I can still see him with the one bulb of his gooseneck fluorescent desk light switched on, scratching away at a tablet with a pencil (like the long black car lady with her checkbook), ripping out a page and starting over, ultimately to lay down the entire set of materials, lean back, and declare he was finished. A few days later I would receive this final piece of the legal tablet in the mail with instructions to put it in the computer and make it look good. I inevitably did, returning six or eight copies to him by mail. He, in turn, would distribute them to the sources he selected, frantically calling to ask for more copies as his audience demanded.

Above that austere, low lit, and often cluttered desk, on the wall, next to the "Have a Hoe in Your Hand" plaque was another one that read "Too Soon We Are Old and Too Late We Are Smart". Seeing it every day until I finally left for college, I often wondered about what it really meant. In retrospect, and seeing the years of writing and creativity that happened at that desk, I am confident that the former is true but that the latter is not.

Hedge (March 1998)

by

Myron S. Nixon

This plant was found growing in the neighborhood of Joplin, Missouri and Tulsa, Oklahoma. It was called *Modoc* or *Modock* by the Osage Indians in that area. Other names are 'Osage Orange', 'Boxwood' and the common name 'hedge'. It is thought that the migrating people from northern Europe brought this name with them because it resembled the common hedge that encircled the manors, estates and castles in Europe.

I shall, for the sake of using the name I grew up with, call it plain 'hedge' throughout this writing. The botanical name is *Maclura pomifera* and it is a distant relative of the mulberry (*Morus*).

The wood has a bright orange color, it splits easily and is covered with thorns throughout. It was a valuable clone in the life of immigrant settlers who used it by encircling there cropland in order to keep livestock from eating their growing crops.

The plant is dioecious, bearing male flowers in racemes and female flowers in heads. The male flowers have a four parted calyx and four stamens; the female flowers have a four cleft calyx and a solitary pistil. Flowers of both sexes lack petals. The osage orange was widely cultivated in the warmer parts of the US as a hedge tree; its wood was used for fence posts.

Hedge fence posts have an oil that resists rot and have been known to last, and still be service free, for 60 to 75 years. White oak, mulberry and black locust, the next best choices, will last only about 8 to 10 years. Line posts are cut to a length of 7 feet and are set about 2.5 feet in the ground and 4.5 feet above the ground for the woven wire to be attached to. Corner posts and gate posts are commonly 10 feet long, set 5 feet in the ground and five feet above ground.

Some hundred years ago, hedge nurseries produced tiny hedge sprouts by gathering hedge balls (apples) into a barrel, allowing them to rot, then planting this pulp in rows in the nursery. Great care was taken to keep these rows free of weeds and watering through the hot summer months.

Hedge served wildlife well also. It furnished a haven for birds of all kinds from songbirds to ground birds such as quail, pheasant, etc. Hawks were unable to penetrate thorny branches and rabbits found a haven under the broad expanse of its thorny growth. Blue Jays have a habit of carrying small twigs of hedge to line the outside of their nests. It is thought they do this to repel snakes who often feed on their eggs and young birds. I have sat for many hours with a rifle and shot jays to keep them from nesting in my yard trees. They carry many small twigs with thorns on them and drop a great many to the ground in the process. This is not good for automobile tires, lawn mower tires, and barefoot children. We always used to go barefoot from spring until fall and a blue jay was a hated bird, leading to more and more expressive names for both blue jays and hedge.

I once asked a farmer for permission to hunt on his land, whereby he readily gave his permission and added "help yourself to those apples as you go by". I could find no apples and it took me some time to realize that he had offered me 'hedge apples', as they were called by some old timers.

Another profession emerging from the hedge culture was one called 'laying hedge'. After the hedge became a few years old and about shoulder high it was carefully trimmed. The following year's growth was allowed to grow to about 8 feet. This growth consisted mostly of water sprouts and when they were cut they were carefully pulled down alongside the existing growth. These water sprouts at about the diameter of a broom handle were cut about half way through and continued to grow down there. This job was done with a special knife resembling a corn knife or a machete. This particular knife had a circular crook at the tip of the blade. This crook was used to lay the half cut portions in place and make a 'hog tight' fence.

My grandmother's sister's husband was known as "a good man to lay hedge".

Anytime anyone worked around hedge in any capacity he was subject to damage from the sharp thorns. People lost eyes, were infected by the juice which was similar to poison ivy, and infections from thorn wounds. As the thorn entered the flesh and was pulled out it left a poisonous residue which caused much pain and discomfort. When a thorn entered into the flesh it would invariably cause the tip to break off and remain there when the thorn was removed, often causing infection along with the discomfort.

When one sat down to remove a thorn from his foot he often [invented] a few new names for the already multinomial plant. No Sunday school names. But this once was overheard as an elderly gentleman sat in the extreme rear pew of the church. He wore extremely faded, threadbare and patched overalls. "Lord you've been good to me so far and I am reluctant to ask for more, but if it comes handy for you, I wish you would deliver me completely and positively from having anything to do with a dead hedge".

Some years ago at public farm sales I would sometimes see one of the old knives used to lay hedge. I didn't know then what it was. Now I wish I had purchased one of them, just for old times sake.

The fruit of the hedge was not edible for human consumption, but was eaten by squirrels, ground hogs, rabbits and often by milk cows. It reputedly caused milk cows to go dry and sometimes caused them to die from strangulation as they tried to swallow the whole ball. The balls were about the size of a soft ball, green in color and made up of small cone like segments. These segments were about the size of a quarter pointed to the middle of the ball, and had a small white seed at the center of the ball.

The hedges are mostly gone now as farmers have adapted their lives to only three crops, Corn, Soybeans and Florida.

Another way in which rural people were served by the thorny hedge plants. Every country person knew that when the quails paired off, the whip-poor-wills called and the leaf on the hedge was a big as a squirrels ear, it was time to plant corn.

The Cake (May 2, 1997)

By
Myron S. Nixon

The *Muleman* black walnut is a little black walnut about the size of a filbert and when cracked yields a little heart shaped kernel. The kernel may be recovered whole and intact.

My wife made a cake and set several of these little heart shaped kernels on top of the cake embedded into the frosting.

She took the cake to a party. Lo and Behold when they decided to serve the cake, someone had picked off all of the walnut kernels.

They never learned who did this, but one of the ladies became sick on the way home and they had to stop twice on the road to attend to her.

Now, it seems odd, when the incident was described to me, her sickness seemed almost identical to a sickness I suffered several times as a boy from eating too many black walnuts.

A coincidence, I'm sure. Yeah, must have been a coincidence.

Chesterfield, Illinois
May 2, 1997

The Quick Change (April 15, 1997)

by
Myron S. Nixon

As I sat resting in my favorite lawn chair, my little three year old granddaughter climbed up on my lap, gave me a big hug and snuggled down on my lap. She was the picture of total and complete complacency. She looked up and said "Grandpa when I get big lets you and me get married. Then we could live like this forever". I replied "That sure sounds great to me. But I can't help but think that if all the little girls married their grandpas, those little boys would have no little girls to play with. They would be sad indeed". She replied that there were no little boys here. "No, not right now" I said "but only about a half hour ago a little boy came by here looking for a little girl to play with". She quickly slid down from my lap, looked around and said "Grandpa, which way did he go?"

Chesterfield, Illinois
April 15, 1997

Reading the Alton Telegraph (July 26, 1997)

Quite noticeable in the Readers Forum is the contrast of opinions about the ink used to print the Alton Telegraph.

Some say it is too light and hard to read. Others proclaim it to be too dark and rubs off on the reader's hands. Two good rules to follow might be proclaimed:

   1. Never read the Telegraph while wearing a white shirt!

   2. Always wash hands with soap and water immediately after reading the Telegraph!

And then there was the lady with identical twin sons. She never could tell them apart. Then they grew up. One became a coal hauler and was grimy and black with coal dust all the time. The other one became an avid reader of the Alton Telegraph. She still can't tell them apart!

Myron S. Nixon
Chesterfield, Illinois
July 26, 1997

Thomas (January 1998)
by
MYRON NIXON

Diagonally across the street from me lived a widow. She had a whole yard full of cats. Among those cats was a jumbo sized, white, tomcat.

One day I happened to notice that white tomcat lying on top of my bluebird house. He was trying to reach into the box to catch the hen bluebird building a nest there.

The wind was blowing hard and making lots of noise, and I decided to sneak up behind Thomas and attach a spring loaded clothes pin onto his tail.

When I made contact with the clothes pin, Thomas immediately went airborne. When he hit the ground, he had his four on the floor working for him, and with a long yodel moved out as if he had suddenly thought of some where else he wanted to be.

Then I heard a loud "Bang" as the widow opened her front door and the wind jerked her storm door out of her hands and slammed it against her house.

The sound of tinkling glass blended well with the yodeling of Thomas in the far distance.

The next day I went over and offered to repair the widow's storm door. All I got was a cold, icy stare, and another cold, icy stare from Thomas as he reclined in the flower bed.

It was then that I noticed something unusual about Thomas. As he lay there he had his tail tucked neatly under his body!

Thomas was taking no chances on a repeat performance!

Chesterfield, Illinois
January 1998

The Smart Cat

My friend's name was Milburn and we called him Meb.

Meb told me this story a long time ago.

Meb had two old bachelor uncles, his father's brothers. They lived down the road a piece and I occasionally went home with them sometimes staying all night.

Being of German ancestry they loved cheese and often brought Limburger cheese. After much persuasion, Meb agreed to try some. He took a bite and almost instantly became sick. He then ran outside and spit it out.

Needing some fresh air he sat down at the wood pile to rest and get some fresh air.

As he sat there an old cat came sauntering along and smelling the cheese he went directly to it sniffed it as few times, dug a hole and buried it.

IX. ALL GRANDPA! ALL THE TIME!

When we lost our Mother in mid June of 1996, I think that of all the family, it affected Dad the most. His health began to fail; he became lethargic and disinterested in things around him. Seeing this, in 1997 my wife and I left the four corners area and moved back to Illinois. We rented a place in south Springfield, situated about forty five minutes from the Chesterfield homestead. We visited him every weekend, working around the farm, planting and tending the annual sweet corn crop, cooking something for him to eat during the coming week, and sitting with him in the lawn chairs in the front yard, in his office.

Within a year, his attitude and his health improved. His humor recovered, he began to tell stories again and even to write a few things. Even so, his health did not allow him to maintain his acreage or his trees, although he tried. My wife and I incorporated in Springfield then and worked a few jobs in the Midwest; we both had backgrounds there. The local archaeological discipline, however, was glutted and it was difficult to break into lifelong networks of local people. We had, after all, been gone for many years, years in which local talent had entrenched themselves in the museums, the universities, the government agencies, and the local private firms. Lacking local support, by necessity we searched for other employment options. That search ended with acceptance of a position in Hemet, in southern California. With strong regrets, we left for the west coast after a little over a year in Illinois.

Not long after that, Dad's health deteriorated again, this time with more serious physical ramifications. The final result of this was to place him in the Heritage Manor Home in Carlinville, Illinois, twelve miles east of Chesterfield. We returned from California and my sister came back from Georgia as often as we could to visit with him and insure that he had the things he needed. On October 14, 2000, at 2:35 PM (Pacific Time) we received a phone call from my sister who informed us that Dad had passed away.

Services were on October 19, 2000, in his beloved Chesterfield; I present the details below. Per his wishes, we buried his remains at Loomis Cemetery just southeast of town. Kindly, and in recognition of his service to his country years before, the local veterans assembled a detail to bid him a military farewell. His marker is a brown granite stone on the northeast segment of the cemetery. Our mother and his wife, Faye, lies next to him. His Granddaughter, Gwen, the one he recalled on his lap, wrote him a last note, reprinted below, as *All Grandpa! All the Time!*

In the early years, prior to college, Dad took a special interest in growing blackberries. As far as I know, he started with wild berries and through grafting, hybridizing, and selecting for the best of each year's crop, he eventually developed a blackberry with a fruit that expanded from the dime sized wild berry to a fruit fully the size of a quarter that grew on a thornless cane that often reached five to six feet in length, and produced gallons of berries each year. With his berries, you could fill your bucket quickly even if you were the oldest child.

When we were in Springfield, I promised a mutual friend from work that I would take her to Dad's farm to pick blackberries when they ripened. Somewhat grudgingly, and out of a sense of kindness, she finally agreed to do so. On arrival, she saw the berries, marveled at their productivity, stationed herself opposite the row from me and kept up with me as we ate our way to the other end. Forget the stains and the thorns, ignore the bugs, and eat your fill. Her original act of simple courtesy had changed to a purple stained face now lighted up with a broad smile.

> "Everything will be right
> And we'll all take delight
> When we turn a stranger into a friend".

On more than one occasion I asked Dad why he did not market these berries. He responded that anyone who wanted some could come and get them on their own, as long as they did not mention insurance or liability. In his mind, it was enough to have developed these delightful berries and to make them available to friends and neighbors; he did not have a profit motive. I do note that now similar varieties are available in the popular seed catalogs, marketed by others with a more developed profit motive than Dad. That was his way.

Through no conscious action on my part or on his, Dad became indirectly dependent on computers. As mentioned above, when he completed writing a piece on that legal pad he kept on his desk, he would mail it to us, we would type in into our computer, and would send him enough copies to satisfy whatever audience he wanted. He liked the professional look of his writing cleaned up with a word processor and printed neatly on the page.

He knew about e.mail through one of his best friends, Jack Sullivan. Jack and Dad shared many botanical interests. Jack had a computer and was probably the only guy in Chesterfield to be on line at the time. Jack also had an e.mail account and at one point, I sent Dad an e.mail through Jack who delivered the hard copy to him. As far as I know, this was Dad's only e.mail ever, but to listen to him it was old hat – as he would tell you, he was in electronic communication with his readers! Thanks, Jack, for making that happen.

Next, an anonymous author wrote a short description of Dad's life. Apparently the author wrote it based on an interview with Dad because it contains details that only he would know and that he would emphasize. When complete, staff posted it on the wall in the nursing home. I include it as a summary of who and what he was as written by someone else.

The final piece is interesting. Someone who used the name "Fluffybunny" as an e.mail address wrote this piece. It came to me in the mail from Jack. The author describes his purchase of a box of original early *Pomona* issues (at a yard sale?), his reading them, and his reaction to the content and flavor of these early works. This narrative concludes with "Fluffybunny's" appraisal of the founding fathers of NAFEX, their attitudes, their ideas, and their ideals.

Concluded,
December 26, 2003,
and again in 2006,
and again in 2007,
and submitted (finally) in 2009,
his son,
Joseph M. Nixon, Ph. D., RPA
Hemet, California

Memorial Service: Myron Stanley Nixon (October 19, 2000)

Burial: Loomis Cemetery
Clergy: Rev. George St. Germain
Pallbearers: Joe Nixon, Clay Guthrie, Jack Sullivan, David Kannallakan

In Loving Memory of
Myron S. Nixon

Date of birth:
November 25, 1919

Date of Death:
October 14, 2000

Survived by:
Son: Joseph Nixon

Daughter:
Gale Guthrie

Grandchildren:
Clay & Dawn Guthrie
Melissa & Cerene Nixon
Gwen Murray

Great Grandchildren:
Krystal, Alex & Kendall Nixon

Sisters:
Ruby Long & Melba Phelps

Funeral Service:
Thursday, October 19, 2000
2:00 PM
Davis-Anderson Funeral Home
Chesterfield, Illinois

Correspondence, October 19, 2000 (Granddaughter Gwen)

Dearest Grandpa:

This, my last note to you, is the hardest to compose. I want to be insightful and witty but find myself languishing in grief. You would admonish me not to wallow in this emotion, but to pick myself up, brush myself off, and get back to it because there are things to be done, but I miss you terribly.

I apologize for being less than attentive in the recent past, but I hope you understand my inability to see you as you were. The weakened and fragile condition of your physical body was the antithesis of anything you ever wanted and I couldn't bear to face the reality and finality of it.

You were such an amazing soul. I loved and admired you so much for always making me feel extraordinary. The other grandkids all had special talents that set them apart. I never felt I was as special as they were except when I was with you. You believed I was exceptional and made me believe it, too. You had a way of making my youthful feelings of inadequacy melt away.

I also thank you for your unwavering support. We disagreed in the past about the level of credit you should receive for my success but I remain steadfast in my belief that you were fundamental. You supported my educational endeavors emotionally and financially. You remained concerned with my intellectual and moral growth. I hope I have made you proud and continue to do so. I strive to carry out my life with the integrity and vitality which came so easily to you.

While your physical absence will be unceasingly felt by me, I am overjoyed that you now walk with me, that I carry you inside me, and I have unlimited access to you. Please watch over me and continue to guide me now as you have done for so long.

All My Love,

Gwen

Just like on MTV: All Grandpa! All the time!

Heritage Manor "Hall of Fame"

Heritage manor of Carlinville has announced a new program, the "Hall of Fame". They display pictures along with short articles describing the past of these certain individuals. Periodically, staff members of Heritage select residents they would like to see honored. Three residents are generally selected for the Hall of Fame and displayed to family and friends in the front foyer. The photographs are given to the family of each resident after the quarter ends as a keepsake.

This quarter Heritage Manor honors Regina Dona, Myron Nixon and Hazel Gracey.

Myron Nixon was born November 25, 1919 in rural Carlinville to Harley and Viola Nixon. Myron has two sisters, Ruby Long and Melba Phelps. Myron's father passed away when he was only two.

Myron's favorite past time of hunting began at ten years of age with trapping. He enjoyed hunting quail with his two English Setters and trapping mink on into his adulthood.

Myron had a very interesting and diverse lifestyle. He spent four years in the Army, stationed both in the US as well as abroad during World War II. Here is where he had the privilege of shaking hands with Ernest Hemingway in Macon, Georgia. Myron resided in the Fiji Islands, as well, for one year and learned to speak their native language fluently. He states he always had an interest in foreign languages and therefore began studying. When he was finished he could speak not only the language of the Fiji Islands but also Spanish, German and Polish. He also travelled to Australia, New Zealand and China.

Myron married and had two children, Gale Guthrie of Georgia and Joseph Nixon of California. When it came time for Myron's children to attend college, he was determined for them to graduate. When push came to shove, Myron made a deal. If they went, he would go. His children did graduate with his daughter becoming a school counselor and his son becoming an anthropologist. After his children graduated, Myron enrolled at Lewis and Clark, with the intention of completing one class which quickly turned into much more. In 1980, Myron graduated from Southern Illinois University with a BA in Liberal Studies.

Myron also enjoyed horticulture. He became president of the Fruit Dabbers Association as well as President of the Illinois Nut Growers Association. He developed a black walnut that you can crack and get out of the shell whole!

Myron was a postal carrier for thirty years in and around Chesterfield. He has five grandchildren and three great grandchildren. He continues to enjoy reading and the company of his family today.

Requiem for A Legacy?
(Anonymous 2003)

The Fluffy Bunny <fuwafuwausagj@muchomail.com>

A few years back I purchased some old issues of Pomona; the $50.00 I paid was a rather cheap price for the education I received in politics, humanity, and not surprisingly - but of perhaps the least significance - fruit cultivation. I'll let you all ponder that one for a moment, but I suspect that those who were around back then kind of know what I am talking about.

Be that as it may, I must confess, it is with a certain amount of anxiety that I approach some of these old issues. You see, in general the NAFEX members of that period were a different sort of folk. Well, perhaps there is the same sort of folks now, but for some reason they are quieter. Many of them wrote with a certain passion, but the most striking thing to me was how they shared from their hearts. I suspect that for many, they were just darned glad they found a group of like-minded folks who cared more about their society than their place in society, who felt a duty to till the earth to glorify their relationship to the Creator, and in the words of my dear friend Ozzie, they "cared more about having a friend than having a buck."

I mention this because several of the Pomona writers of old wrote less about growing, varieties, or cultivation, and more about the nostalgia they felt and the connection with departed family members they experienced when they were tilling the earth. There exists a sense of profoundness in their words as they recounted their memories of an age that I, frankly, never experienced, and a state of innocence I suppose I never had. That world just doesn't seem to exist anymore, but to hear of it, it sure must have been a fine place. These days the Politically Correct crowd has folks afraid to mention the name of the Lord, yet those old NAFEXers proclaimed His glory in many of their writings.

I mentioned that I read these old, most precious issues with a sense of apprehension; that apprehension stems from the sorts of emotions those NAFEXers conveyed through some of their writings. I must confess that, from time to time, a tear wells up in my eye when I read some of their words; I certainly feel a sense of loss that I never had the privilege of meeting such fine people, and I feel a sense of loss for our society due to its change in culture. Three of my favorite old time NAFEXers who never fail to tug at my emotional cords are: Myron Nixon, Eugene Griffith, and Brooks D. Drain.

In July of 1969, Myron Nixon recounts the lessons learned at the knee of his beloved grandmother as he states: I once asked my beloved grandmother this same question, Why plant this tree?" The answer I got is still stamped in my memory as if it were yesterday (Nixon 1969). She told of hunger and poverty in Europe, of starvation and oppression. She told of crossing the great ocean at nine years old, of a baby sister who died at sea, and of a terrible storm that damaged the rigging of the ship and which forced them to stay "a long time at a terrible cold place."

"Then her face lit up, and she smiled as she told of landing here and coming to central Illinois. She told of the great forest of nuts and berries to be had for the picking, and of such bountiful harvest beyond her wildest dream. Someone had planted all of this for her, she had said, and she lived in great abundance for nearly 70 years. Now, she said, we must plant more so you and your children will have plenty in times to come. At ten, it was hard for me to envision ever being seventy, but it gave me a warm feeling inside to think that we were planting trees for me; and I remember as I washed up for supper that evening my mother asked me if I had been helping Grandma. I replied ,no, mama; Grandma has been helping me."

As I read more of Mr. Nixon's writings, the values his beloved grandmother instilled in him showed through: honesty, selflessness, and a love of others permeated his works. It is hard to imagine a man paying a greater tribute to those who raised him than to so closely mirror their values.

In 1971 Mr. Griffith spoke plainly, his love of humanity and compassion for others shining through when he stated: The question I am asked most frequently is, "How are you going to keep others from using your invention if you succeed...? (Griffith 1971). The answer is simple-and perhaps I am simple, too-but my present thinking is, I'm not even going to try. I know I'm church-mouse poor and enjoy creature comforts as much as anyone, but age-wise I'm beyond trying to make a million, for I haven't found a way of taking it with me. I have no objection to making a dime or two now and then, especially as it helps buy gas for some ideas I currently have on the back burner for lack of financial fuel. My reward, and I would find it most gratifying, would be in knowing that a hungry mother and child in Appalachia, in Brazil, in India, in Africa, or anywhere...might eat better and suffer less because of my efforts.

My only regret-and this is no plea for help, [for as] much as I sometimes think I'd like it, I can't bring myself to ask for nor accept it-is that I'm always a dollar short, and perhaps ultimately, a day late. I pass here only once. I'd like to help even, perhaps undeserving humanity, just this wee bit.

I have no idea whatever happened to Mr. Griffith, but as his words were penned some thirty-three years past, I suspect that he has passed this earthly plane. It is hard for me to imagine that Mr. Griffith did not find his riches in the afterlife; I wish I had had the chance to know a man like that; I am a lesser man for lack of that experience.

Brooks D. Drain relates, A long time ago, I was a little boy and was looking out of windows in my father's home . . . and saw a young pear . . . dying in our yard. I was told that it had some disease and that this had gone on since the early settlers had come to America. This disease, later called fireblight...

Mr. Drain then relates his lifelong dedication to trying to find and produce blight-resistant pears, and dispenses advice on treatment advice, as well as harvesting advice freely . . . but most astonishing is the ending of his article. I let Mr. Drain tell you in his own words:

The writer is an old man approaching 80 years of age. Do not expect me to do too much, but I hope the rest of you can make things so little boys and girls can look out of windows in their homes and see pears of quality growing and fruiting...may God bless the little boys and little girls.

Today, we as a society are an educated lot: perhaps not in the classical sense, but most of us can certainly put a pen to paper-okay, now I have revealed my true age, for who among us does not have access to a word processor these days? Ahh...now you see where I am going. I am ashamed to have to hear our diligent editor Jackie Kuehn "beg" for submissions to Pomona. I cannot help but wonder if this is how we show our appreciation for the legacy handed to us by NAFEX's founders? Of course, I find a touch of irony in the fact that, in scanning old issues of "the" Pomona, frequent reference was made to having to severely edit material for lack of space, and out and out decline to publish submissions for a plethora of reasons. I hope many of you will reflect on the selflessness of NAFEX's heritage and pay homage to that spirit by filling future issues of Pomona. I would certainly love to hear about what you grow, your trials and errors, how you work with your children tilling the earth, how your grandma taught you, but mostly I would like to hear some passion from the ranks, something that tells me NAFEX's spirit is still alive.

In closing, I'll just say that I feel blessed to have had my life enriched by the words of those whom tread this earth before me. Our Founders in NAFEX have left us a rich legacy, a richness that I cannot help but feel is not fully appreciated by many.

Excelsior,
The Fluffy Bunny

X. REFERENCES CITED

Anonymous. 2003. *Requiem for a Legacy?* Pomona, The Journal of the North American Fruit Explorers. Summer 2003, Pp. 6-9.

Griffith, Eugene. 1971. *I Pass Here Only Once*, The North American Pomona, Quarterly Journal of The North American Fruit Explorers, Vol. IV No.3, July. Pp. 81-82.

Harding, A. R. 1906. *Fox Trapping*. Columbus, Ohio: A. R. Harding Publisher.

Nixon, Myron S. 1998. "Hedge". In Nixon, Joseph M., M. Colleen Hamilton, Albert H. Brine and Colleen M. Clark. 1998. *Final Report of Phase I Archaeological Survey of Upland Agricultural Areas Belonging to Commonwealth Edison, Inc. within the Sensitivity Zone Surrounding Sangchris Lake, Christian and Sangamon Counties, Illinois.* Prepared for Commonwealth Edison, Inc., Chicago, Illinois. Prepared by White Oak Environmental Alliance, Inc., San Jacinto, California. June.

Nixon, Myron. 1969. *Why Plant That Tree?* North American Pomona No.8, July. Pp. 1-2.

Index